Space
to Imagine

Study Creative Writing at Bath Spa

The Creative Writing Centre at Bath Spa University has been helping people get published for over three decades. We are now accepting applications for Autumn 2011 entry on the following programmes of study:

MA Creative Writing

MA Writing for Young People

MA Scriptwriting

MA in Travel & Nature Writing*

PhD in Creative Writing – full time and now with brief and no residency options*

www.bathspa.ac.uk/schools/humanities-and-cultural-industries/creative-writing

* Subject to approval

GRANTA

12 Addison Avenue, London W11 4QR

email editorial@granta.com

To subscribe go to www.granta.com

Or call 845-267-3031 (toll-free 866-438-6150) in the United States, 020 8955 7011 in the United Kingdom

ISSUE 114: WINTER 2011

EDITOR	John Freeman
DEPUTY EDITOR	Ellah Allfrey
ARTISTIC DIRECTOR	Michael Salu
ONLINE EDITOR	Ollie Brock
ASSISTANT EDITOR	Patrick Ryan
EDITORIAL ASSISTANT	Yuka Igarashi
PUBLICITY	Saskia Vogel
DESIGN INTERN	Francesca Ulivari
FINANCE	Geoffrey Gordon, Morgan Graver, Craig Nicholsc
MARKETING AND SUBSCRIPTIONS	Anne Gowan, David Robinson
SALES DIRECTOR	Brigid Macleod
SALES MANAGER	Sharon Murphy
TO ADVERTISE IN THE UK CONTACT	Kate Rochester, katerochester@granta.com
TO ADVERTISE IN THE USA CONTACT	Emily Cook, ecook@granta.com
IT MANAGER	Mark Williams
PRODUCTION ASSOCIATE	Sarah Wasley
PROOFS	Sarah Barlow, Kelly Falconer, Katherine Fry, Jessica Rawlinson, Vimbai Shire
PUBLISHER	Sigrid Rausing

Refugees shouldn't be forced to scavenge to survive.

Thousands of asylum seekers in the UK are denied employment, made homeless, refused healthcare and rely on handouts to survive.

It's time to treat refugees as people.

Support our campaigns and you could put an end to this scandalous destitution. Please make a stand and donate to the Refugee Council today.

PROTECTING REFUGEES FOR **60** YEARS

Visit **www.refugeecouncil.org.uk**
Phone 020 7346 1205

UK Reg. Charity No. 1014576

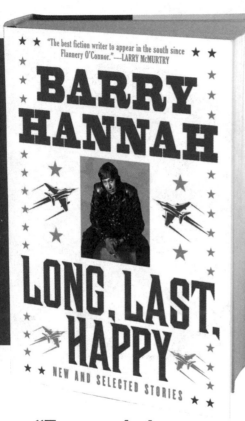

CONTENTS

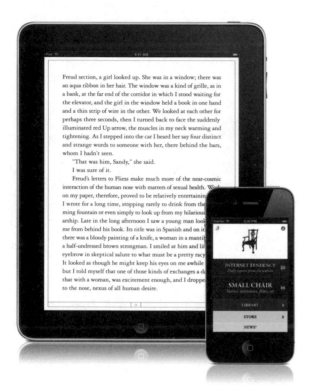

COME, JAPANESE!

Julie Otsuka

On the boat we were mostly virgins. We had long black hair and flat wide feet and we were not very tall. Some of us had eaten nothing but rice gruel as young girls and had slightly bowed legs, and some of us were only fourteen years old and were still young girls ourselves. Some of us came from the city, and wore stylish city clothes, but many more of us came from the country and on the boat we wore the same old kimonos we'd been wearing for years – faded hand-me-downs from our sisters that had been patched and re-dyed many times. Some of us came from the mountains and had never before seen the sea, except for in pictures, and some of us were the daughters of fishermen who had been around the sea all our lives. Perhaps we had lost a brother or father to the sea, or a fiancé, or perhaps someone we loved had jumped into the water one unhappy morning and simply swum away, and now it was time for us, too, to move on.

On the boat the first thing we did – before deciding who we liked and didn't like, before telling each other which one of the islands we were from, and why we were leaving, before even bothering to learn each other's names – was to compare photographs of our husbands. They were handsome young men with dark eyes and full heads of hair and skin that was smooth and unblemished. Their chins were strong. Their posture, good. Their noses were straight and high. They looked like our brothers and fathers back home, only better dressed, in grey frock coats and fine Western three-piece suits. Some of them were standing on sidewalks in front of wooden A-frame houses with white picket fences and neatly mowed lawns, and some were leaning in driveways against Model T Fords. Some were sitting in studios on stiff high-backed chairs with their hands neatly folded and staring straight into the camera, as though they were ready to take on the world. All of them had promised to be there, waiting for us, in San Francisco, when we sailed into port.

On the boat we often wondered: Would we like them? Would we love them? Would we recognize them from their pictures when we first saw them on the dock?

On the boat we slept down below, in steerage, where it was filthy and dim. Our beds were narrow metal racks stacked one on top of the other and our mattresses were hard and thin and darkened with the stains of other journeys, other lives. Our pillows were stuffed with dried wheat hulls. Scraps of food littered the passageways between berths and the floors were wet and slick. There was one porthole and in the evening, after the hatch was closed, the darkness filled with whispers. *Will it hurt?* Bodies tossed and turned beneath the blankets. The sea rose and fell. The damp air stifled. At night we dreamed of our husbands. We dreamed of new wooden sandals and endless bolts of indigo silk and of living, one day, in a house with a chimney. We dreamed we were lovely and tall. We dreamed we were back in the rice paddies, which we had so desperately wanted to escape. The rice paddy dreams were always nightmares. We dreamed of our older and prettier sisters, who had been sold to the geisha houses by our fathers so that the rest of us might eat, and when we woke we were gasping for air. *For a second I thought I was her.*

Our first few days on the boat we were seasick and could not keep down our food, and had to make repeated trips to the railing. Some of us were so dizzy we could not even walk and lay in our berths in a dull stupor, unable to remember our own names, not to mention those of our new husbands. *Remind me one more time, I'm Mrs Who?* Some of us clutched our stomachs and prayed out loud to Kannon, the goddess of mercy – *Where are you?* – while others of us preferred to turn silently green. And often, in the middle of the night, we were jolted awake by a violent swell and for a brief moment we had no idea where we were, or why our beds would not stop moving, or why our hearts were pounding with such dread. *Earthquake*, was the first thought that usually came to our minds. We reached out for our mothers then, in whose arms we had slept until the day we'd left home. Were they sleeping now? Were they dreaming? Were they thinking of us all the time? Were they still walking three steps behind our fathers on the streets with their arms full of packages while our fathers carried nothing at all? Were they secretly envious of us for sailing away? *Didn't I give you everything?* Had they remembered to air out our old kimonos? Had they remembered to feed the cats? Had they made sure to tell us everything we needed to know? *Hold your teacup with both hands, stay out of the sun, never say more than you have to.*

Most of us on the boat were accomplished, and were sure we would make good wives. We knew how to cook and sew. We knew how to serve tea and arrange flowers and sit quietly on our flat wide feet for hours, saying absolutely nothing of substance at all. *A girl must blend into a room: she must be present without appearing to exist.* We knew how to behave at funerals, and how to write short, melancholy poems about the passing of autumn that were exactly seventeen syllables long. We knew how to pull weeds and chop kindling and haul water and one of us – the rice miller's daughter – knew how to walk two miles into town with an eighty-pound sack of rice on her back without once breaking into a sweat. *It's all in the way you breathe.* Most of us had good manners and were extremely polite, except for when we got mad and cursed like sailors. Most of us spoke like ladies most of the time, with our voices pitched high, and pretended to know much less than we did, and whenever we walked past the deckhands we made sure to take small, mincing steps with our toes turned properly in. Because how many times had our mothers told us: *Walk like the city, not like the farm!*

On the boat we crowded into each other's bunks every night and stayed up for hours discussing the unknown continent ahead of us. The people there were said to eat nothing but meat, and their bodies were covered with hair (we were mostly Buddhist, and did not eat meat, and only had hair in the appropriate places). The trees were enormous. The plains were vast. The women were loud and tall – a full head taller, we had heard, than the tallest of our men. The language was ten times as difficult as our own and the customs were unfathomably strange. Books were read from back to front and soap was used in the bath. Noses were blown on dirty cloths that were stuffed back into pockets only to be taken out later and used again and again. The opposite of white was not red, but black. What would become of us, we wondered, in such an alien land? We imagined ourselves – an unusually small people armed only with our guidebooks – entering a country of giants. Would we be laughed at? Spat on? Or, worse yet, would we not be taken seriously at all? But even the most reluctant of us had to admit that it was better to marry a stranger in America than grow old with a farmer from the village. Because in America the women did not have to work in the fields and there was plenty of rice and firewood for all. And wherever you went the men held open the doors and tipped their hats and called out, 'Ladies first,' and 'After you.'

Some of us on the boat were from Kyoto, and were delicate and fair, and had lived our entire lives in darkened rooms at the back of the house. Some of us were from Nara, and we prayed to our ancestors three times a day, and swore we could still hear the temple bells ringing. Some of us were farmers' daughters from Yamaguchi with thick wrists and broad shoulders who had never gone to bed after nine. Some of us were from a small mountain hamlet in Yamanashi and had only recently seen our first train. Some of us were from Tokyo and had seen everything, and spoke beautiful Japanese, and did not mix much with any of the others. Many more of us were from Kagoshima and spoke in a thick southern dialect that those of us from Tokyo pretended we could not understand. Some of us were from Hokkaido, where it was snowy and cold, and would dream of that white landscape for years. Some of us were from Hiroshima, which would later explode, and were lucky to be on the boat at all though of course we did not then know it. The youngest of us was twelve, and from the eastern shore of Lake Biwa, and had not yet begun to bleed. *My parents married me off for the betrothal money.* The oldest of us was thirty-seven, and from Niigata, and had spent her entire life taking care of her invalid father, whose recent death made her both happy and sad. *I knew I could only marry if he died.* One of us was from Kumamoto, where there were no more eligible men – they had all left the year before to find work in Manchuria – and felt fortunate to have found any kind of husband at all. *I took one look at his photograph and told the matchmaker, 'He'll do.'* One of us was from a silk-weaving village in Fukushima, and had lost her first husband to the flu, and her second to a younger and prettier woman who lived on the other side of the hill, and now she was sailing to America to marry her third. *He's healthy, he doesn't drink, he doesn't gamble, that's all I needed to know.* One of us was a former dancing girl from Nagoya who dressed beautifully, and had translucent white skin, and knew everything there was to know about men, and it was to her we turned every night with our questions. How long will it last? With the lamp lit or in the dark? Legs up or down? Eyes open or closed? What if I can't breathe? What if I get thirsty? What if he is too heavy? What if he is too big? What if he does not want me at all? 'Men are really quite simple,' she told us. And then she began to explain.

On the boat we sometimes lay awake for hours in the swaying damp darkness of the hold, filled with longing and dread, and wondered how we would last another three weeks.

On the boat we carried with us in our trunks all the things we would need for our new lives: white silk kimonos for our wedding night, colourful cotton kimonos for everyday wear, plain cotton kimonos for when we grew old, calligraphy brushes, thick black sticks of ink, thin sheets of rice paper on which to write long

letters home, tiny brass Buddhas, ivory statues of the fox god, dolls
we had slept with since we were five, bags of brown sugar with which
to buy favours, bright cloth quilts, paper fans, English phrase books,
flowered silk sashes, smooth black stones from the river that ran
behind our house, a lock of hair from a boy we had once touched, and
loved, and promised to write, even though we knew we never would,
silver mirrors given to us by our mothers, whose last words still rang
in our ears. *You will see: women are weak, but mothers are strong.*

On the boat we complained about everything. Bedbugs. Lice.
Insomnia. The constant dull throb of the engine, which
worked its way even into our dreams. We complained about the
stench from the latrines – huge, gaping holes that opened out on
to the sea – and our own slowly ripening odour, which seemed to
grow more pungent by the day. We complained about Kazuko's
aloofness, Chiyo's throat-clearing, Fusayo's incessant humming of
the 'Teapicker's Song', which was slowly driving us all crazy. We
complained about our disappearing hairpins – who among us was
the thief? – and how the girls from first class had never once said
hello from beneath their violet silk parasols in all the times they had
walked past us up above on the deck. *Just who do they think they
are?* We complained about the heat. The cold. The scratchy wool
blankets. We complained about our own complaining. Deep down,
though, most of us were really very happy, for soon we would be in
America with our new husbands, who had written to us many times
over the months. *I have bought a beautiful house. You can plant tulips
in the garden. Daffodils. Whatever you like. I own a farm. I operate
a hotel. I am the president of a large bank. I left Japan several years
ago to start my own business and can provide for you well. I am 179
centimetres tall and do not suffer from leprosy or lung disease and there
is no history of madness in my family. I am a native of Okayama. Of
Hyogo. Of Miyagi. Of Shizuoka. I grew up in the village next to yours
and saw you once years ago at a fair. I will send you the money for your
passage as soon as I can.*

On the boat we carried our husbands' pictures in tiny oval lockets that hung on long chains around our necks. We carried them in silk purses and old tea tins and red lacquer boxes and in the thick brown envelopes from America in which they had originally been sent. We carried them in the sleeves of our kimonos, which we touched often, just to make sure they were still there. We carried them pressed flat between the pages of *Come, Japanese!* and *Guidance for Going to America* and *Ten Ways to Please a Man* and old, well-worn volumes of the Buddhist sutras, and one of us, who was Christian, and ate meat, and prayed to a different and longer-haired god, carried hers between the pages of a King James Bible. And when we asked her which man she liked better – the man in the photograph or the Lord Jesus Himself – she smiled mysteriously and replied, 'Him, of course.'

Several of us on the boat had secrets, which we swore we would keep from our husbands for the rest of our lives. Perhaps the real reason we were sailing to America was to track down a long-lost father who had left the family years before. *He went to Wyoming to work in the coal mines and we never heard from him again.* Or perhaps we had left behind a young daughter who had been born to a man whose face we could now barely recall – a travelling storyteller who had spent a week in the village, or a wandering Buddhist priest who had stopped by the house late one night on his way to Mount Fuji. And even though we knew our parents would care for her well – *If you stay here in the village*, they had warned us, *you will never marry at all* – we still felt guilty for having chosen our own life over hers, and on the boat we wept for her every night for many nights in a row and then one morning we woke up and dried our eyes and said, 'That's enough,' and began to think of other things. Which kimono to wear when we landed. How to fix our hair. What to say when we first saw him. Because we were on the boat now, the past was behind us, and there was no going back.

On the boat we had no idea we would dream of our daughter every night until the day that we died, and that in our dreams she would always be three and as she was when we last saw her: a tiny figure in a dark red kimono squatting at the edge of a puddle, utterly entranced by the sight of a dead floating bee.

On the boat we ate the same food every day and every day we breathed the same stale air. We sang the same songs and laughed at the same jokes and in the morning, when the weather was mild, we climbed up out of the cramped quarters of the hold and strolled the deck in our wooden sandals and light summer kimonos, stopping, every now and then, to gaze out at the same endless blue sea. Sometimes a flying fish would land at our feet, flopping and out of breath, and one of us – usually it was one of the fishermen's daughters – would pick it up and toss it back into the water. Or a school of dolphins would appear out of nowhere and leap alongside the boat for hours. One calm, windless morning when the sea was flat as glass and the sky a brilliant shade of blue, the smooth black flank of a whale suddenly rose up out of the water and then disappeared and for a moment we forgot to breathe. *It was like looking into the eye of the Buddha.*

On the boat we often stood on the deck for hours with the wind in our hair, watching the other passengers go by. We saw turbaned Sikhs from the Punjab who were fleeing to Panama from their native land. We saw wealthy White Russians who were fleeing from the revolution. We saw Chinese labourers from Hong Kong who were going to work in the cotton fields of Peru. We saw King Lee Uwanowich and his famous band of gypsies, who owned a large cattle ranch in Mexico and were rumoured to be the richest band of gypsies in the world. We saw a trio of sunburned German tourists and a handsome Spanish priest and a tall, ruddy Englishman named Charles, who appeared at the railing every afternoon at quarter past three and walked several brisk lengths of the deck. Charles was travelling in first class, and had dark green eyes and a sharp, pointy nose, and spoke perfect Japanese, and was the first white person many of us had ever seen. He was a professor of foreign languages at the university in Osaka, and had a Japanese wife, and a child, and had been to America many times, and was endlessly patient with our questions. Was it true that Americans had a strong animal odour? (Charles laughed and said, 'Well, do *I*?' and let us lean in close for a sniff.) And just how hairy *were* they? ('About as hairy as I am,' Charles replied, and then he rolled up his sleeve to show us his arms, which were covered with dark brown hairs that made us shiver.) And did they really grow hair on their chests? (Charles blushed, and said he could not show us his chest, and we blushed and explained that we had not asked him to.) And were there still savage tribes of Red Indians wandering all over the prairies? (Charles told us that all the Red Indians had been taken away, and we breathed a sigh of relief.) And was it true that the women in America did not have to kneel down before their husbands or cover their mouths when they laughed? (Charles stared at a passing ship on the horizon and then sighed and said, 'Sadly, yes.') And did the men and women there really dance cheek to cheek all night long? (Only on Saturdays, Charles explained.) And were the dance steps very difficult? (Charles said they were easy, and gave us a moonlit lesson in the foxtrot the following evening on the deck. *Slow, slow, quick, quick.*) And was downtown San Francisco truly bigger than the Ginza? (Why, of course.) And were the houses in America really three times the size of our own? (Indeed they were.) And did each house have a piano in the front parlour? (Charles said it was more like every other house.) And did he think we would be happy there? (Charles took off his glasses and looked down at us with his lovely green eyes and said, 'Oh, yes, very.')

Some of us on the boat could not resist becoming friendly with the deckhands, who came from the same villages as we did, and knew all the words to our songs, and were constantly asking us to marry them. We already *are* married, we would explain, but a few of us fell in love with them anyway. And when they asked if they could see us alone – that very same evening, say, on the 'tween deck, at quarter past ten – we stared down at our feet for a moment and then took a deep breath and said, 'Yes,' and this was another thing we would never tell our husbands. *It was the way he looked at me,* we would think to ourselves later. Or, *He had a nice smile.*

One of us on the boat became pregnant but did not know it and when the baby was born nine months later the first thing she would notice was how much it resembled her new husband. *He's got your eyes.* One of us jumped overboard after spending the night with a sailor and leaving behind a short note on her pillow: '*After him, there can be no other.*' Another of us fell in love with a returning Methodist missionary she had met on the deck and even though he begged her to leave her husband for him when they got to America she told him that she could not. 'I must remain true to my fate,' she said to him. But for the rest of her life she would wonder about the life that could have been.

Some of us on the boat were brooders by nature, and preferred to stay to ourselves, and spent most of the voyage lying face down in our berths, thinking of all the men we had left behind. The fruit seller's son, who always pretended not to notice us, but gave us an extra tangerine whenever his mother was not minding the store. Or the married man for whom we had once waited, on a bridge, in the rain, late at night, for two hours. And for what? A kiss and a promise. 'I'll come again tomorrow,' he had said. And even though we never saw him again we knew we would do it all over in an instant, because being with him was like being alive for the very first time, only better. And often, as we were falling asleep, we found ourselves thinking of the peasant boy we had talked to every afternoon on our way home from school – the beautiful young boy in the next village whose hands could coax up even the most stubborn of seedlings from the soil –

and how our mother, who knew everything, and could often read our mind, had looked at us as though we were crazy. *Do you want to spend the rest of your life crouched over a field?* (We had hesitated and almost said yes, for hadn't we always dreamed of becoming our mother? Wasn't that all we had ever once wanted to be?)

O n the boat we each had to make choices. Where to sleep and who to trust and who to befriend and how to befriend her. Whether or not to say something to the neighbour who snored, or talked in her sleep, or to the neighbour whose feet smelled even worse than our own, and whose dirty clothes were strewn all over the floor. And if somebody asked us if she looked good when she wore her hair in a certain way – in the 'eaves' style, say, which seemed to be taking the boat by storm – and she did not, it made her head look too big, did we tell her the truth, or did we tell her she had never looked better? And was it all right to complain about the cook, who came from China, and only knew how to make one dish – rice curry – which he served to us day after day? But if we said something and he was sent back to China, where on many days you might not get any kind of rice at all, would it then be our fault? And was anybody listening to us anyway? Did anybody care?

S omewhere on the boat there was a captain, from whose cabin a beautiful young girl was said to emerge every morning at dawn. And of course we were all dying to know: was she one of us, or one of the girls from first class?

O n the boat we sometimes crept into each other's berths late at night and lay quietly side by side, talking about all the things we remembered from home: the smell of roasted sweet potatoes in early autumn, picnics in the bamboo grove, playing shadows and demons in the crumbling temple courtyard, the day our father went out to fetch a bucket of water from the well and did not return, and how our mother never mentioned him even once after that. *It was as though he never even existed. I stared down into that well for years.* We discussed favourite face creams, the benefits of leaden powder, the first time we saw our husband's photograph. *He looked like an earnest person, so I figured he was good enough for me.* Sometimes we found ourselves saying things we had never said to anyone, and once we got started it was impossible to stop, and sometimes we grew suddenly silent and lay tangled in each other's arms until dawn, when one of us would pull away from the other and ask, 'But will it last?' And that was another choice we had to make. If we said yes, it would last, and went back to her – if not that night, then the next, or the night after that – then we told ourselves that whatever we did would be forgotten the minute we got off the boat. And it was all good practice for our husbands anyway.

A few of us on the boat never did get used to being with a man, and if there had been a way of going to America without marrying one, we would have figured it out.

On the boat we could not have known that when we first saw our husbands we would have no idea who they were. That the crowd of men in knit caps and shabby black coats waiting for us down below on the dock would bear no resemblance to the handsome young men in the photographs. That the photographs we had been sent were twenty years old. That the letters we had been written had been written to us by people other than our husbands, professional people with beautiful handwriting whose job it was to tell lies and win hearts. That when we first heard our names being called out across the water one of us would cover her eyes and turn away – *I want to go home* – but the rest of us would lift our heads and smooth down the skirts of our kimonos and walk down the gangplank and step out into the still warm day. *This is America,* we would say to ourselves, *there is no need to worry.* And we would be wrong. ∎

Write
in Miami!

The Writers Institute

a creative writing conference
of the Florida Center for the Literary Arts
at Miami Dade College

Four days of intensive workshops on fiction, nonfiction, poetry and more—all taught by renowned authors. Plus manuscript consultations, pitch sessions with agents and editors, networking events and more!

Mark your calendars:

May 4 - 7, 2011

For registration, manuscript submission deadlines, and more information visit **www.flcenterlitarts.com** or call **305.237.3940**.

Florida Center
for the **Literary Arts**
at Miami Dade College

Miami Dade
College

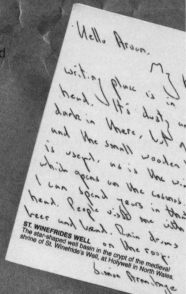

BEACH

Roberto Bolaño

Fiction translated from the Spanish by Natasha Wimmer

I gave up heroin and went home and began the methadone treatment administered at the outpatient clinic and I didn't have much else to do except get up each morning and watch TV and try to sleep at night, but I couldn't, something made me unable to close my eyes and rest, and that was my routine, until one day I couldn't stand it any more and I bought myself a pair of black swimming trunks at a store in the centre of town and I went to the beach, wearing the trunks and with a towel and a magazine, and I spread my towel not too far from the water and then I lay down and spent a while trying to decide whether to go into the water or not, I could think of lots of reasons to go in but also some not to (the children playing at the water's edge, for example), until at last it was too late and I went home, and the next morning I bought some sunscreen and I went to the beach again, and at around twelve I headed to the clinic and got my dose of methadone and said hello to some familiar faces, not friends, just familiar faces from the methadone line who were surprised to see me in swimming trunks, but I acted as if there was nothing strange about it, and then I walked back to the beach and this time I went for a dip and tried to swim, though I couldn't, and that was enough for me, and the next day I went back to the beach and put on sunscreen all over and then I fell asleep on the sand, and when I woke up I felt very well rested, and I hadn't burned my back or anything, and this went on for a week or maybe two, I can't remember, the only thing I'm sure of is that each day I got more of a tan and though I didn't talk to anyone each day I felt better, or different, which isn't the same thing but in my case it seemed like it, and one day an old couple turned up on the beach, I remember it clearly, it looked like they'd been together for a long time, she was fat, or round, and must have been about seventy, and he was thin, or more than thin, a walking skeleton, I think that was why I noticed him, because usually I didn't take much notice of the people on the beach, but I did notice them, and it was because the guy was so skinny, I saw him and got scared, fuck, it's death coming for me, I thought, but nothing was coming for me, it was just two old people, the man maybe seventy-five and the woman about seventy, or the other way around, and she seemed to be in good health, but he looked as if he were going to breathe his last breath any time now or as if this were his last summer, and at first, once I was over my initial fright, it was hard for me to look away from the old man's face, from his skull barely covered by a thin layer of skin, but then I got used to watching the two of them surreptitiously, lying on the sand, face down, with my face hidden in my arms, or from the boardwalk, sitting on a bench facing the beach, as I pretended to brush sand off myself, and I remember that the old woman always came to the beach with an umbrella, under which she quickly ducked, and she didn't wear a bathing suit, although sometimes I saw her in a bathing suit, but usually she was in a very loose summer dress that made her look fatter than she was, and under that umbrella the old woman sat reading, she had a very thick book, while the skeleton that was her husband lay on the sand in nothing but a tiny swimsuit, almost a thong, and drank in the sun with a voracity that brought me distant memories of junkies frozen in blissful immobility, of junkies focused on what they were doing, on the only thing they could do, and then my head ached and I left the beach, I had something to eat on the Paseo Marítimo, a little dish of anchovies, and a beer, and then I smoked a cigarette and watched the beach through the window of the bar, and then I went back and the old man and the old woman were still there, she under her umbrella, he exposed to the sun's rays, and then, suddenly, for no reason, I felt like crying and I got in the water and swam and when I was a long way from shore I looked at the sun and it seemed strange to me that it was there, that big thing so unlike us, and then I started to swim toward the shore (twice I almost drowned) and when I got back I dropped down next to my towel and sat there panting for quite a while, but without losing sight of the old couple, and then I may have fallen asleep on the sand, and when I woke up the beach was beginning to clear, but the old man and the old woman were still there, she with her novel under the umbrella and he on his back in the sun with his eyes closed and a strange expression on his skull-like face, as if he could feel each second passing and he was savouring it, though the sun's rays were weak, though the sun had already dipped behind the buildings along the beach, behind the hills, but that didn't seem to bother him, and then I watched him and I watched the sun, and sometimes my back stung a little, as if that afternoon I'd burned myself, and I looked at them and then I got up, I slung my towel over my shoulders like a cape and went to sit on one of the benches of the Paseo Marítimo, where I pretended to brush non-existent sand off my legs, and from up there I had a different vision of the couple, I said to myself that maybe he wasn't about to die, I said to myself that maybe time didn't exist in the way I thought it existed, I reflected on time as the sun's distance lengthened the shadows of the buildings, and then I went home and took a shower and examined my red back, a back that didn't seem to belong to me but to someone else, someone it would still be years before I got to know, and then I turned on the TV and watched shows that I didn't understand at all, until I fell asleep in my chair, and the next day it was back to the same old thing, the beach, the clinic, the beach again, a routine that was sometimes interrupted by new people on the beach, a woman, for example, who was always standing, who never lay down in the sand, who wore a bikini bottom and a blue T-shirt, and who when she went into the water only got wet up to the knees, and who was reading a book, like the old woman, but this woman read it standing up, and sometimes she knelt down, though in a very odd way, and picked up a big bottle of Pepsi and drank, standing up, of course, and then put the bottle back down on the towel, which I don't know why she'd brought since she never lay down on it or went swimming, and sometimes this woman scared me, she seemed too strange, but most of the time I just felt sorry for her, and I saw other strange things too, all kinds of things happen at the beach, maybe because it's the only place where we're all half naked, though nothing too important ever happened, once as I was walking along the shore I thought I saw an ex-junkie like me, sitting on a mound of sand with a baby on his lap, and another time I saw some Russian girls, three Russian girls, who were probably hookers and who were talking on a single cellphone and laughing, all three of them, but what really interested me most was the old couple, partly because I had the feeling that the old man might die at any moment, and when I thought this, or when I realized I was thinking this, crazy ideas would come into my head, like the thought that after the old man's death there would be a tsunami and the town would be destroyed by a giant wave, or that the earth would begin to shake and a massive earthquake would swallow up the whole town in a wave of dust, and when I thought about what I've just described I hid my head in my hands and began to weep, and while I was weeping I dreamed (or imagined) that it was night-time, say three in the morning, and I left my house and went to the beach, and on the beach I found the old man lying on the sand, and in the sky, up near the stars, but closer to earth than the other stars, there shone a black sun, an enormous sun, silent and black, and I went down to the beach and lay on the sand too, the only two people on the beach were the old man and me, and when I opened my eyes again I realized that the Russian hookers and the girl who was always standing and the ex-junkie with the baby were watching me curiously, maybe wondering who that weird guy was, the guy with the sunburned shoulders and back, and even the old woman was gazing at me from under her umbrella, interrupting the reading of her interminable book for a few seconds, maybe wondering who that young man was, that man with silent tears running down his face, a man of thirty-five who had nothing at all but who was recovering his will and his courage and who knew that he would live a while longer. ∎

WALKING ON THE WEST BANK

Robert Macfarlane

M y questioner cannot understand the stones.
'Why are you bringing these to Israel?'

She holds out the two flints. One has complicated surface patterns of petrol blue and foxy red. I think: it resembles a map. I think: perhaps she imagines the stone is an illicit map of some kind that I am trying to smuggle into the country? I am not thinking straight.

'I like stones,' I say. 'I collect them. I've brought these as gifts.'

'So you *do* know people here?'

I've made a mistake. It isn't my first. I have been lying persistently and badly for about an hour and a half now, to a variety of interrogators, in a variety of rooms in Tel Aviv airport. The rooms in which I have been questioned have been diminishing in size: entrance hall, side room, back room, booth.

The inquiries continue, looping back over the same ground with minor variations of route, seeking weaknesses in my story. There are plenty of weaknesses.

Where am I staying? Who do I know here? What is the purpose of my visit? What are my plans, exactly, day by day?

I persevere in my poor lies.

The American Colony Hotel, Jerusalem. Nobody. Academic tourism. I plan to visit the Dead Sea, Jaffa, of course Jerusalem. No, I have no intention of visiting the West Bank.

Where am I staying? Who do I know here? What is the purpose of my visit?

So it goes on. I have now assumed that they will not let me into Israel, and that I will be back on a plane to London once they've finished. I no longer mind about this. I just don't want to be in these increasingly small rooms.

Later, another questioner arrives, my fourth. He is a gentle, rubbery-faced man. He doesn't tell me his name, so I think of him as Benjamin. Benjamin is apologetic in his tone, warm in his queries, like a curious friend. I experience a sudden flowering of Stockholm syndrome. I want to tell Benjamin everything: that I am going from Tel Aviv to the West Bank, that I will be staying in Ramallah with a well-known Palestinian writer and human rights lawyer, and that we will be conducting a series of day-long walking trespasses within restricted-access Zone C landscapes. I almost tell Benjamin these things, then I stick to my answers, red-faced and sweating.

As unexpectedly as it began, it ends. Many people trying to enter or leave through Tel Aviv have had much worse. I repack my bags. Benjamin escorts me out of the booth, through the back room and into the entrance hall, before pointing the way to the exit. He apologizes for the mild inconvenience. He hopes I understand the situation, the necessity. He wishes me a good stay in Israel.

I leave, trying to walk confidently, truthfully, on my jelly legs: like a drunk driver attempting to pace off the road dashes to prove his sobriety. I imagine that there is a path ahead of me on the glossy tiled floor which I must keep to, and this steadies my gait a little.

Tel Aviv, on the Mediterranean coast of Israel, and Ramallah, in the central West Bank, are thirty-six beeline miles apart. About forty-five minutes' drive on a direct road. But to get to Ramallah while avoiding Israeli checkpoints requires a circuitous approach perhaps three times as long, passing through villages and along thin roads. The terrain is of winding terraced hills of limestone, ceding to marly chalk. I reach Ramallah just as darkness falls. Piles of rubble and rubbish on its outskirts. Jasmine, lemon and bougainvillea line the streets. Hooded crows scavenge in the trash heaps, making two-footed hops. From the jasmine there is a scent of jasmine, from the lemon trees a scent of lemon, from the vegetable shops the smell of green, and from the trash heaps the smell of shit.

Posters on walls and telephone poles advertise 'The 29th Basketball Match of the Martyrs'. Spray-can graffiti tags in green, red and black fill most available wall space. The bougainvillea is just on the turn and is shedding white petals like tiny vellum pages, which flock in their hundreds of thousands on the pavements and around the bases of trees.

Later, Raja – the friend I am visiting – drives me up to an unlit road that runs along the high ground on the south-west of Ramallah. From the road edge, the land falls steeply away in terraces. We get out, and stand looking across.

'This is where we will walk from tomorrow,' says Raja. The valley at our feet is in darkness. Beyond it is a strange pattern of lights. Nearest to us, at our altitude, are squashed ellipses of light with ribbons of paired lights swooping up to them. Between the ellipses, but lower, are untidy neon scatters. Further away, in the distance, a clean curve of sodium orange, hemmed with absolute darkness. To me, an unreadable map of sight- and light-lines.

'Twelve in that direction alone,' Raja says.

'Twelve?'

'Settlements. The rings of light are the Jewish settlements, on the hilltops, with the well-lit roads leading up to them. The smaller messes of light, lower down, are the Palestinian villages. The curve beyond them is the lights of the coast of what is now Israel. The darkness is the Mediterranean. That is Jaffa, where my family lived before the *Nakba*.'

It is all so small in scale, absurdly small. I think: you can look from the middle of the West Bank right across Israel to the Mediterranean. I could throw a stone from here into the nearest settlement.

Raja Shehadeh has been walking the hills of Ramallah for more than forty years. When he began walking, before the Six Day War of 1967, the appearance of the hills was largely unchanged from the time of the Roman occupation, and it was possible to walk more or less unimpeded among them: to conduct what in Arabic is known as a *sarha*.

In its original verb form, *sarha* meant 'to let the cattle out to pasture early in the morning, allowing them to wander and graze freely'. It was subsequently humanized to suggest the action of a walker who went roaming without constraint or fixed plan. One might think the English equivalent to be a 'stroll', an 'amble', or a 'ramble', but these words don't quite catch the implications of escape and of improvisation, of re-creation rather than recreation, that are carried by *sarha*. 'Wander', perhaps, is the closest we have, a word shadowed by wonder.

Since 1967, and the occupation of the Palestinian territories by Israel, Raja has watched the open landscape around Ramallah and throughout the West Bank increase in fragility and diminish in size. It has become gradually more difficult to find paths which are not cut across by a settlers' bypass road, which do not lead too close to a training area for Palestinian militia, or to an Israeli army post. The Israeli settlement policy in the West Bank brought with it a lavish road-building project, with the use of the new roads usually restricted to Israelis, and their routes secured by the army. Ramallah, too, has sprawled as a city, eating up more and more of the landscape around it. Palestinian planning regulations are restrictive with regard to building materials (all new-builds must be in limestone) but lax with regard to location (anywhere you like).

So the *sarha* has become almost impossible. Hills that had once been the setting for an experience of freedom have come to feel endangered and endangering. But Raja still walks. A minimum of once a week, usually more. As walking has become less easy, it has become correspondingly more important: a way of defeating the compression of space of the occupation. A small but repeated act of civil disobedience. Occasionally, Raja tells me, walking allows him briefly to forget the occupation. He speaks of the euphoria at being out beyond checkpoints and walls and barriers, of feeling 'giddy with joy' under a wide-open sky. Sometimes the evidence of deep time, of the spans of geological history, the knowledge that he is walking the limestone bed of an ancestral sea, laid down at a rate of about 1mm per century, over a period of about thirty-five million years, crushes his frustrations at the Palestinian predicament to a wafer.

Raja is neat, small, bird-like. He is precise in his movements and his speech. When he is looking for the right word, he rubs his forefinger and thumb together as if crumbling something friable, reducing it to finer units. When he is thinking about something he tilts his head very slightly to one side. A comment which requires no response from him will be met with none. It takes me some time to interpret his silence not as a reprimand, but merely as an efficiency. His modesty is formidable, and entirely uncontrived. He has none of the English modesty which knowingly depresses evidence of achievement in order that it might spring out more forcefully at some future point.

'It will be necessary to be vigilant tomorrow,' Raja says, as we stand looking out over the darkness and the light. 'Down there' – he gestures into the valley – 'is where Penny and I were pinned down by gunfire, behind a boulder.' I have heard about this incident. Raja and his wife had been walking during the wild early years of the second intifada, when bullets suddenly struck the rock above their heads. They sheltered while ricochets and rock splinters hissed around them. It had been Palestinian auxiliaries, practising their aim, choosing live targets.

There had been other frightening encounters. Palestinian villagers who thought Raja was an Israeli settler. Israeli settlers who thought Raja was a Palestinian villager. Three years ago, while out walking with an English friend, Louisa, he had been confronted by two young Palestinian men, unidentifiable beneath their keffiyehs. They were carrying cudgels. They had said: 'Except for you, we would slaughter her immediately,' pointing to Louisa.

The next morning, not long after dawn, we leave from Raja's house to begin the first of our walks, down a long curling valley, Wadi 'qda, which trends westwards, towards the coast. We drop off the edge of the high road and along a poorly tarmacked track that hairpins down the terraced slope. I can tell Raja is anxious, and I can tell that he wants to disguise his anxiety from me.

Almost immediately, a bad omen. After three bends in the track, we reach a thin breeze-block wall, plastered with cement. It has been turned into a firing range. Targets have been scratched on to the plaster: concentric circles plugged by bullet holes. Green glass bottles are lined up along the top of the wall. Most have had their tops shot off. I start humming 'Ten Green Bottles' to myself. The song will buzz like a fat fly in my brain for the rest of the day.

'Militants, or police?' I ask.

'Could be either. Probably police.' It is only over the past three years or so that an effective Palestinian police force has been established, reclaiming most of the West Bank towns from armed gangs. They need somewhere to train.

A hundred yards further on, the road runs out, the tarmac dribbling to a stop next to a part-completed villa. We move on to rough ground and pick up a path that descends the terracing, towards the wadi bed. The heat of the day is building, but a big westerly wind is also blowing. At the base of an olive tree, I find a scatter of dozens of big bullet casings. They look like the spoor of a creature: AK-47 droppings.

The terraces are thick with vegetation. Big holm oaks here and there among the olive trees. Bryony with its baroque-heart leaves snaking up stands of teasel: botanical rhymes with the chalklands of south-east England. Marjoram, sage, thyme and hyssop. And everywhere is *natsch*, a scrubby, spiny thistle that grows to ankle height. The existence of *natsch* has been used by Israeli land lawyers as a floral shorthand for waste ground – evidence that an area of land is not being farmed or used. Once designated as unused, the area of land can then be reclassified as 'public' land and then more easily requisitioned when necessary. Everything here intersects with politics.

Land in the West Bank is zoned by the Israelis into three areas: A, B and C. A is for the major Palestinian towns and cities. B is for the villages. The rest of the West Bank, the open country, is C, and is out of bounds to Palestinians. Raja tells me this with some relish when we step into Zone C, and become trespassers according to Israeli law.

Nine green bottles, standing on the wall. A big dog fox breaks cover on the other side of the valley, vaults downhill for a few metres, disappears into rocks. After a mile or so of moving along the terraces we come to a stone tower, made out of limestone that has been tanned by marl to a yellowish brown. This is a *qasr*, a small tower used as a base by farmers and shepherds. They dot the hills. Most are dilapidated. This one is intact, and corbelled. It reminds me of the beehive shielings of south Lewis and north Harris in the Outer Hebrides. I drop to my hands and knees and crawl in through the narrow doorway. Raja comes in after me.

'Actually, it is a good idea to offer warning of coming,' he says, his voice echoey in the cool space. 'Throw a stone in first, so that any snakes or scorpions will retreat. You can think of it as a gesture of politeness, like knocking on a door.'

Raja is a good route-finder. Over the decades of *sarha*, he has gained, as he puts it, 'an eye for the ancient tracks that criss-cross the hills, like catwalks'. Near the *qasr*, he picks up an obviously old path which leads down to the floor of the valley, the dry wadi bed. There, the path merges with the wadi, following the natural line in the landscape for both walkers and water. We pass coils of barbed wire, snaking out of the silt on the wadi floor. More bullet casings. Reminders that this valley was fought over in 1967; that Ramallah was besieged and bombarded as recently as 2003.

As we walk the wadi path, Raja begins to tell me stories. He speaks about the people he has brought here, and what the experience of the landscape has done to them. He speaks about the different seasons of colour in the valley: now it is yellow and purple. He points out a stand of dark finger-like cypresses perhaps two miles away, rare strong verticals in this lateral landscape.

'For years it was impossible to come into this valley because the army was stationed where those cypresses are,' he says. 'They surveyed the valley and would intercept anyone walking here. Now they've moved closer to Dolev, so we are able to walk here again.'

Eight green bottles, standing on the wall. A pair of kestrels mews and spins in the air on the far side of the valley. As I turn to watch them, a pair of gazelles – the same browns and tans as the hillside

– appears below the kestrels. The gazelles are up and running, flowing uphill, seemingly without using their legs, like a kind of counter-gravitational fluid.

Then – men are watching us. Palestinian men, from a roadside, perhaps half a mile away. They have turned towards us, are talking. Raja watches them watching us, but doesn't say anything to me. He just alters our route slightly, heading further uphill and away from them. I feel exposed, scrutinized, and am filled with the ridiculous worry that I might lose my footing, stumble and accidentally fall.

Travellers to the Holy Lands have always moved through a landscape of their imagination. The land itself has been easily forgotten (sloughed off as inconvenient or irrelevant) or dismissed (as lifeless and repugnant). Again and again, Western pilgrims, surveyors and cartographers found the same qualities in the Palestinian hills: barrenness, the macabre. William Thackeray came to Palestine in the 1840s and dismissed the countryside as 'parched', 'savage', 'unspeakably ghastly and desolate', a place marked only by 'fear and blood, crime and punishment', a terrain of sustained sanguinary rites. 'There is not a spot at which you look but some violent deed has been done there, or some massacre has been committed,' he wrote. To Herman Melville, a decade later, the limestone resembled an ossuary spread over thousands of square miles: the hills of 'whitish mildew . . . bleached-leprosy-encrustations of curses-old cheesebones of rocks, crunched, gnawed and mumbled'.

For Raja, walking is a way to refute these illiterate readings of his hills, a method of telling and discovering stories other than those of murder and sterility. He dislikes using maps when he walks, partly because map reading could be mistaken for a suspicious action, but more importantly because each official map has its own colonial history of self-interest and misreading (British Ordnance Survey, Israeli). Raja prefers to build up what he calls his 'map in the head', signposted by personal memories and references. He shows me a map he has made of the Ramallah hills and wadis. It is marked with naive drawing-doodles, specific place names in Arabic (of escarpments, outcrops, wadi outfalls), and little captions in English. 'Where Penny and Raja came under gunfire.' 'Where Aziz [Raja's nephew] picked up the unexploded missile.' 'Where I encountered the Israeli settler with a gun.' 'Where Abu Ameen has his qasr.' 'That rock where Jonathan and I stopped and had a long talk.' 'Where I found the dinosaur footprint.'.

To walk between such places is for Raja to join events up into stories. Recording his walks, he is creating his own songlines, of thin silk, preserving at least in language what is vanishing in materiality. The paths he follows possess a near-supernatural quality: he tells me of hearing voices in the *qasrs*, of seeing faces at dusk in the limestone outcrops.

L ater. Miles further down the valleys, we have left Wadi 'qda and entered Wadi Kalb. The village of A'yn Qenya is to our north-west and beyond that, on the hilltop barely half a kilometre away, the Israeli settlement of Dolev, with its army post and watchtower guarding the entrance. The sky has become heavy with unseasonal rain. The air is close, tense. So is the landscape.

Suddenly there is a crackle. A boom echoes across the valley. I think: this is the first peal of thunder. I think: that was a bomb. No, a feedback screech follows. It is the static of the loudspeakers from the A'yn Qenya mosque being turned on. A silence, and then a voice, furiously emphatic, begins to shout. *God is Great! God is Great! Muhammad is his prophet! Alluhu Akbar!*

It is the Friday sermon. Eight loudspeakers mounted on the mosque tower, two in each window, pointing to each cardinal point. Raja sighs neatly.

'There did not used to be this zealousness to the sermons. But now, of course, as there is so little pleasure in this life, the only hope is in the next. People have become disaffected, and as they have done so, the sermons have become angrier.'

We step over two dead dogs, flattened into the ground. I stop to look at them, distracted by the fabulous mycelial landscape of mould that has sprung up on their pelts.

'In Ramallah now, I cannot sleep through the 4 a.m. sermon. The imam becomes crazier and crazier, and then everyone complains, and he calms down for a while, and then he forgets and becomes crazy again.'

We pick our way up through terraces of prickly pears. Terrace walking is like upwards pachinko. You move along, and then where the land offers you an option – a slope-spill of soil from one terrace down to the next; a protruding boulder – you ascend. Along, up, left and along, up, right and along, making for the next ascent point. Terraces of olive, lemon, orange and pomegranate, the pomegranates overripe, splitting lavishly on the branch. Around the foot of the trunk is litter. Flattened bottles: Sprite, Coke, mineral water. Also turds: human turds, horse turds, sheep turds, dog turds.

The imam rants and raves. *Of the best deeds are the unity of Muslim in general and of Palestinians in particular! Do not be like those who thrive in disputes for they will be severely punished!* I think: it is hard, here, to find anywhere that is out of earshot of a mosque tower and out of gunshot of an army tower.

Rain begins to fall. The droplets are the biggest I have ever seen, leaving splash marks on the limestone the size of two-pound coins. Because of the westerly wind, the splash marks are elliptical rather than circular. The arrangement of the drops relative to one another is also peculiar: they appear to be spaced according to a rough, regular geometry. To my eye they seem to fall in a formation of interlocking squares, falling at four corners. It seems almost that the rain is leaving corridors down which we can walk without getting struck.

When the drops hit me, they land and crack like little eggs breaking on the head. The rain makes the chalky marl soil sticky as treacle. In under a minute, Raja and I both have bulbous cakes of yellow mud on the soles of our shoes, leaving our feet heavy as a deep-sea diver's boots. The rain wakes the scent of the sage. The rain also wakes the smell of decaying animal flesh and human shit, overpowering the sage.

'Let's run for the villa,' Raja says, beginning to march smartly up the path we have now picked up. The villa is perhaps a hundred yards up the slope. Raja has told me about it. Until 1967 the villa belonged to the Zalatimo family, well known in Palestine as pastry-makers. After the occupation, they were forced to leave.

A big terrace blocks my view of the villa, but I know roughly where it is. The rain is pummelling down, so I think I will take a short cut. I scramble up a limestone buttress of the big terrace, and freeze.

A man is running across the open ground in front of the house, making for cover. He is not Raja. Inside the villa I see another man. He is wearing some sort of webbing and strapping. Something metal is slung across his front; it glints.

I drop back down behind the limestone terrace. I think: I know I have been seen. I think: they must be either settlers or soldiers. I have to stop Raja. I run uphill after him, past a vast holm oak, but see him already moving along the path to the house.

He has almost reached the front door. I think: he can't have seen that there are people inside. He opens the door. There is a shout. One of the men moves quickly towards Raja. And embraces him. I hear Raja exclaim, 'Basel!' Then, 'What luck!'

The first thing I see as I go inside is a horse. The back double doors of the house are wide open, and a white horse is standing perfectly centred in the threshold, looking over its shoulder at me. There are also five people: three men, two women. One of the men, who is clearly Raja's friend, has a baby in a carrier with glinting metal buckles slung on his front.

Astonishingly, it is the Zalatimo family themselves, who have come back to see their ancestral villa. 'I try to come here once a month or so,' says Basel, Raja's friend who lives in Jerusalem. 'This is my mother, who has not been back here for many years, and this is my aunt, making her last visit.' A look passes between Basel and his mother. The aunt smiles broadly and nods a greeting to Raja and me.

The family abandoned the villa in 1967. It is now a wreck. Fangs of glass in the windows. The floor thick with dust, pine needles and holm-oak acorns. The walls dense with graffiti. The villa, visited both by Dolev settlers and local villagers, has become a site of textual dispute. Crude black drawings of AK-47s spitting out bullets at a spray-painted Star of David. A swastika. A heart, dripping black blood. Many Romanized names that mean nothing to me, and many Arabic and Hebrew texts that I cannot read.

The big central hall opens to two domed-roof rooms, set either side of the hall. I scuff away the dust from a section of the floor with my foot, feeling a glossy surface beneath, and reveal intact floor tiles marked with black diagonals that interlock. Basel's mother comes over to me.

'These are a very special surface,' she says apologetically, as though the tiles have been left dirty for a day, rather than forty-two years. 'You need only to wipe them with a mop and – they gleam as though they've been waxed!' She gestures me outside, to the front balcony of the house, and with a revelatory sweep of her arm, like a magician releasing an armful of doves, indicates the landscape in front of us. The air smells of pine resin. 'To me, there is no finer view in the world!' I see arid terracing and olive trees. I see the Dolev settlement away to the west. I see the village, with its trash slews spilling from its lower edges. I wonder what she is seeing.

She tells me that she left Palestine in 1959 for Kuwait, and then for America. She rarely returns. She steers me back inside, and gives me a tour of the house, as if I am the first visitor since a recent refurbishment.

'This is where we piled the sacks of flour,' gesturing to one corner of the hall, 'and here where we piled the sacks of rice.'

In the corner of one of the rooms, Basel is busy measuring up windows with a tape measure.

'You will not find windows that fit!' says his mother. 'All windows are different! I tell you, no two windows are the same!'

Basel snicks a button on the tape measure with his thumb. The measure flickers back into its housing like a snake's tongue, with a skittery sound.

'Let's just see, Mother. I'll bring them up from home, see if they fit. It would be the first stage.'

Basel's mother steps close to me, and opens her hand like a conjuror about to blow magic dust, or revealing a coin plucked from behind an ear. Two knobbly brown pebbles sit in her palm.

'I could not resist, I have taken two more.'

'Not *more*, Mother,' says Basel from the other room.

'You would like to come and see the bread oven my father and uncle built.' I agree that I would, so she leads me out of the back door of the house, past the horse, in the rain, along a muddy path.

'Watch that you do not slip on the mud,' she says. I grip her elbow so that she does not slip on the mud.

'Come, come, and here it is.' I am expecting a vast stone oven; a blast furnace, built into the hillside. In fact, it is a small rusty carcass, barely recognizable as an oven, with an L-shaped mouth.

'This is how it opens,' she says, creaking back the bent door to the thing. As she does so, she angles her face away, as if avoiding a rush of hot air. The interior is filled with brown pebbles.

'This is where the pebbles come from?'

'Yes, many from here, a whole bag, I took other stones from Hebron, Haifa, Jericho, Jerusalem, one or more from every part of Palestine. I took these stones home and laid them on the belly of my oven in America, and I bake my bread on them, so that when I lift the loaf up once it is baked, Palestine has left its mark on the belly of the bread. You can get this kind of bread in Ramallah; it is called *taboun*. I recommend it!'

Her brow furrows. 'The Israelis have stolen this land from us, they are thieves. I once wrote a letter to Ronald Reagan, I knew it would go in the waste-paper basket, but I needed to get it off my chest. "Dear President Reagan," it began . . .'

I stop listening. Down in the valley, a covey of partridges breaks from cover and whirrs, churring, across the far flank of the valley.

A man comes out of a house on the lower side of the village and hurls a bucketful of rubbish down the hillside.

'This is my aunt's last visit here,' Basel says to me as we are about to leave. 'But she remembers this place and that is good. At the King Hussein Bridge they gave her one week on her visa, though she had a multi-entry document. We've outstayed the visa by two weeks. It doesn't matter. Her Alzheimer's is too bad.'

The aunt smiles at me. The thunder crashes. The donkey brays. The rain pours. A drill thumps like gunfire. Somewhere higher up the valley the wadi starts to run with water, and the path we have walked becomes a river.

The following day, we walk again. This time Raja and I are accompanied by a German geologist called Clemens Messerschmid. Truly, this is his name. Messerschmid is tall. His hair is grey and long. Hanks of it fall across his face and he uses his little fingers to tuck them back behind his ears. He walks with a hungry bouncing lope. His passion is geology, and he barely talks about anything else. For years, he has been studying the flow rates of the springs and rivers in Wadi Zarqa. The Israelis do not want him working in the West Bank.

Messerschmid knows everything about the region through which we are walking, near the village of Ras Karkar. He knows every footpath, every side valley, and grades each according to the relative likelihoods of meeting settlers. He also likes to describe the geomorphology of each new area. His language is magnificent, unselfconsciously lyrical. We stop in shade and he draws explanatory diagrams in quick, confident black ink, explaining to me the anticline cross section of the West Bank, the saltwater–sweetwater interface at the Dead Sea coast, the karstified landscape of the Hebron formation, with its Swiss-cheese limestone.

He explains that geologists describe the solvent action of rainwater on limestone as the creation of 'preferential pathways'. With each shower of rain, drops of water are sent wandering across the surfaces of the limestone, etching the track of their passage with acid as they go. These first traverses create tiny shallow channels, which in turn attract the flow of subsequent water, such that they become more deeply scored into the rock. Through the action of water, a hairline crack over time becomes a runnel, which becomes a fracture site, which becomes an escarpment edge.

In a landscape where the limestone is a significant surface formation, these larger-scale fissures are often decisive in the development of terracing and of footpaths. Humans and animals, seeking a route, are guided by the preconfigured habits of the terrain. These walkers create preferential pathways, which in turn attract the flow of subsequent walkers, all of whom etch the track of their passage with their feet as they go. In this way the chance path of a raindrop hundreds of thousands of years previously determines the route of a contemporary walker.

Later, we are walking up a wadi bed towards the refugee camp. The stones of the wadi bed have been rinsed and turned by the intermittent flow of the wadi, so it is like walking a cobbled street. 'These are the most natural paths of the landscape,' says Messerschmid. Its cleaned stones remind me of the Via Dolorosa in Jerusalem, whose stone steps have been polished by the passage of millions of walkers, murmuring stories to themselves as they walk uphill.

I see a rounded lump of chert; bend down and pick it up. It resembles a white eyeball wrapped in layers of brown linen. Messerschmid takes the stone from my hand, eyes it back and weighs it thoughtfully.

'A nice piece of chert, this.'

I tell him about the questioning I received at Tel Aviv concerning my stones. He smiles.

'Ah, well, you know that chert – flint – is the favourite stone of the intifada!' He tosses up the eyeball and catches it again. 'The young Palestinians have told me that chert is their favourite throwing stone, that it makes the best missile. It is sharp-edged, hard and heavy in the hand.'

Messerschmid tucks a hank of hair behind his ears. A bulbul flutters out from a gum tree. Yesterday's rain soaks down through the karstic pipes into the aquifer forty million years beneath our feet.

'Not far from here,' says Messerschmid, 'I once came across two chameleons making love in a fig tree. One of them had turned black, the other had turned red. It was unclear which one was enjoying itself.'

Later, in Wadi Zarqa. Someone has chiselled a trough into the limestone, where the water collects before being piped off to irrigate the terraces. Messerschmid leans over and drinks from a spring with two cupped hands. The terraces here are thick with green growth: snaking vines, chillies, squashes, artichokes.

'They call these the bleeding hills, or the crying hills,' says Messerschmid, pointing to the spring, 'because they weep water. In January, February, when the proper rainfall happens, many springs run here. They are the consequence of the meeting of layers: where karstic limestone encounters marl, the water descends but cannot descend further, and so it ducts itself outwards. The springs run, and the hills weep.' He indicates with his little finger a dark slur of stain on the limestone. 'We call such springs "contact springs". They occur when two different kinds of rock encounter one another, where Hebron meets Yatta, for instance. Permeable and impermeable combine, and the result is a kind of generosity.'

We leave the spring, walk west through hot, still air. Sweat pearls on my eyebrows. We pass stands of eucalyptus with their psoriatic bark, trees introduced by the British during the mandate years of 1921–48. This famously thirsty species was the worst possible choice for a land so poor in water.

As I walk in the heat, the images of the day begin to melt and blur into one another in my mind, politics seeping into geology and vice versa. Generous and ungenerous border encounters. Anticlines and karsts. Preferential pathways, saltwater–sweetwater interfaces, mobilized iron, the collapse of the land, the impossibility of innocent language.

Later. Raja and I are in the open area south of Jerusalem, which Israelis call 'The Judaean Wilderness', but which Raja prefers to call 'The Jerusalem Wilderness'. It is the Empty Quarter of Israel and the West Bank: there are no settlements, no villages. It is too dry and its slopes too steep. After the crush of Ramallah and its environs, the emptiness is a shock to the eye. The hills are of glaring white chalk and limestone, tanned in the lower reaches by marl. This was the region in which many of the desert saints of the fourth to sixth centuries established their monasteries and cells, seeking an abbreviation of eternity in the expanses and silence of the terrain.

We are with a man called Hani, a friend of Raja's who has agreed to drive us. As we near Jerusalem, Hani's mobile phone rings. He answers, tucks the phone between his right shoulder and right ear, tilts his head to trap it in place. His voice turns serious, deeper, and then urgent. Raja listens. The phone call ends. Raja and Hani talk.

The call was from a reporter from Haaretz, the left-wing Jewish news organization, Raja explains, sounding stunned. He was telling Hani that the murderer of Hani's younger brother has been arrested and has confessed – twelve years after the crime. In 1997, Hani's brother had been found dead in his taxi in Jerusalem, shot once through the head. He was twenty-two at the time of his murder. He had been an engineering student, who had taken a part-time job to pay for his studies. For twelve years Hani and his family had known nothing about the circumstances of the murder.

Now, it transpired, the killer was a Jewish settler called Yaakov 'Jack' Teitel who at the time of the killing had been resident in Florida. He had flown to Israel, killed Hani's brother, killed an elderly Palestinian shepherd, and then flown home: murder tourism. He had subsequently returned to Israel and moved into the Shvut Rachel settlement in the West Bank. From there, he had carried out a campaign of bombing and violence against left-wing Jews which had eventually led to his arrest. The previous day, he had confessed to the murders and bomb attacks.

A day later, in East Jerusalem. Raja is no longer with us. Hani pulls the car up to the pavement and turns in his seat to talk to me, looking back over his right shoulder. He tells me that his older brother has gone back to the family home in Ramallah to get photographs of their murdered brother for distribution to the media.

'My brother is so angry,' Hani says.

He looks worried, even hurt, as if this were an improper reaction, somehow indecorous.

'This anger has no point,' he says. 'There is no going back. This is done. Our brother cannot return.

'I just want the same for Israeli as for Arab,' he says. 'He asked me, the reporter, if I see this man Teitel behind me in the street, what do I do? I tell him, if I see him, the settler behind me, I will not try to kill him. The police, they are the people to punish him. But I want one thing, to ask him why, why he killed my brother?'

He is quiet for a few seconds.

'What can you do?'

He is quiet again.

'The reporter told me how the settler shot him. He put the gun here' – Hani cocks his thumb and forefinger, and places the tip of his finger into the rump of bone behind his right ear – 'then he shot him, bang, and the little metal . . .'

I realize he is tailing off for want of language, not emotional stamina.

'Bullet.'

'Bullet. The bullet came out here.'

He bunches the fingertips of his right hand in front of his left eye, and then suddenly splays them apart, jerking his hand away.

I reach out a hand and grip his shoulder in a gesture of comfort. He looks quickly down at my hand as if I am committing an assault. I realize that our physical positions mimic those of Teitel and

Hani's brother, and take my hand away. I realize I don't know Hani's brother's name.

Over Hani's shoulder, up the street, two dumpsters are smouldering, thick black smoke rising in a column. In one, I can see the upper curves of a sofa. A single trainer hangs over the near edge of the other dumpster, hitched by its laces to its invisible partner.

'What can you do,' says Hani. It is not a question. ■

New Hotel Krakow

In February the poplars are even slimmer
than in summer, frozen through. My family
spread across the earth, beneath the earth,
in different countries, poems, paintings.

Noon, I'm on Na Groblach Square.
I sometimes came to see my aunt
and uncle here (partly out of duty).
They'd stopped complaining about their fate,

the system, but their faces looked like
an empty second-hand bookshop.
Now someone else lives in that apartment,
strange people, the scent of a strange life.

A new hotel was built nearby,
bright rooms, breakfasts doubtless comme il faut,
juices, coffee, toast, glass, concrete,
amnesia – and suddenly, I don't know why,
a moment of penetrating joy.

GRANTA

EDENVALE

Mark Gevisser

We brought rings and two witnesses to the Edenvale Home Affairs office because we had been told to.

It was 22 February 2009. I had gone to the office, located on a scrappy strip of motor-repair shops and panel beaters east of Johannesburg, to book our ceremony three weeks previously. My partner, C, and I had been together for nearly two decades, but we had little interest in the rites of marriage. We had decided to do it, now, solely because it would facilitate our move to France, where he had been offered a job. It was, we told each other, merely an administrative matter.

Three years before, the South African parliament had passed a law permitting same-sex marriage, upon injunction from the Constitutional Court. We could have done it more easily – through a gay rabbi I know, for example, or a gay judge who is a friend – but we wanted to see the system work for us. Even though we lived on the other side of town, we chose Edenvale because friends had had a positive experience there. Like all Home Affairs offices, it was grimy and arcane, contemptuous and chaotic; the last place on earth you would want to get married. In the old days, Home Affairs had been the processing room of apartheid: it told you who you were and where you could (and could not) be. It was still a place of profound alienation; of a million frustrations and rages a day.

And I was about to have one of them: I had been waiting in the queue since 2.30 p.m., and had only made it to the front just after 3 p.m. Although the office closed at half past three, processing stopped half an hour before, and I was just too late. I would have to come back the next day. I was on the brink of a spirited lecture on the meaning of '*Batho Pele*', the department's new slogan of 'People First', when one of the women behind the desk looked up at me, gold hoops in her ears to match her attitude, and barked: 'Same sex or opposite sex?'

It took me a moment to comprehend. 'Same sex,' I said, a little too loudly, glancing round to see if any of the other clerks in the room would look up in shock, or perhaps just interest. They did not.

'The marriage officer likes to do the same-sexes early in the morning,' the woman said briskly, consulting her book. 'Too much paperwork, you people. You've made our lives much more difficult.'

Before I could protest, the woman shoved a form across to me, noting the time and date of our appointment. Pulling out a green highlighter, she underlined a reminder that at least two witnesses were required. 'We have room for twenty,' she said, 'so bring all your friends and family.'

'No, no,' I protested. 'It'll be just two. We don't want to make a fuss.'

'Why not?'

When I shrugged and spluttered an answer ('purely an administrative matter'), she looked at me severely. 'A marriage is a big deal. *Make* a fuss. Don't forget the rings.'

We would not be doing rings.

'Why not?' she repeated, before answering her own question: 'Ah, you don't want to make a fuss!' And then, in counselling mode: 'Do you think you are a second-class citizen just because you are gay? You have full rights in this new South Africa. You have the *right* to make a fuss. I think you need to go home, and have a *very serious* chat with your partner. We will see you at 8.30 a.m. on 22 February. With witnesses and rings. Goodbye.'

There I was, an entirely empowered middle-class, middle-aged white man, being lectured by a young black woman about my rights. And here we were three weeks later, with rings but, alas, only two witnesses, being ushered up the stairs by a delightful security guard who told our friend that she was a beautiful bride but who shifted the compliment effortlessly to me when corrected.

We found ourselves in 'Room 8: Marriages' at the back of the building, overlooking a scrapyard next door. It was a parallel universe: the room was draped in lace of the same dead colour palette as the dried wild flowers set in vases between white porcelain swans. There were wedding photos of various couples tacked on to the walls and, on every available surface, cascades of what turned out, on closer inspection, to be empty ring boxes. It was inexplicable at first, then comical, then unexpectedly moving.

'You like it?' trilled a voice behind us. A middle-aged Afrikaans woman had entered. She introduced herself as Mrs Austin; she was actually in finance, but she loved marrying people so much that she had applied for a licence and now did it two mornings a week. 'This is all *my* work,' she said of Room 8, explaining that every couple she married was invited to leave its ring boxes behind, and that among these boxes were 'same-sex' ones: she was proud of the fact that she had married more gay couples than any other officer in the province.

Mrs Austin made no secret of her disappointment at our lack of campery: where were the feathers, the champagne? After some jocularity over who would be the 'man' by signing the register first, she led us through an unmemorably bureaucratic script ending in 'I do' and a kiss before presiding over what was clearly, for her, the more significant part of the proceedings: the swapping of the rings. I slipped on to C's finger a delicate band of red gold fretted in the South Indian style of his ancestors, while he wound on to mine a thick chunk of silver. Exhaling approval, Mrs Austin extracted a red heart-shaped ring box from her installation and balanced it between our two hands, which she delicately arranged for a photograph. We spent more time on this ritual than we had on the actual ceremony, and as we posed I admired the contrasting styles of our rings and what they said about our relationship.

It was, in the end, the lack of moment to it all – the unportentousness, if there is such a word – which finally moved me. Even though Mrs Austin kept referring to us as 'same-sex', and heterosexuals as 'normal', we were swept out of Room 8 on a tide of hilarity and giggled all the way to breakfast. Even the fact that she could not furnish us with a marriage certificate – the computers had been down for six weeks because someone had stolen the cables – did not dampen the good feelings. We were a white man and a black man, free to be together in the country of our birth, treated with dignity and humanity and much good-natured humour by a system that had denied both for so long.

I am forty-six and C is fifty. We live our lives openly; our families and colleagues and neighbours all know that we are gay and together. It is his choice, however, to be private; to remain outside of my public identity. As we drove away I felt, for the first time, what it meant to claim a right once denied, to claim the freedom to choose: the bounds of our privacy, the terms of our public engagement. Well worth the fuss.

On the day of our marriage my father was recovering from surgery. We went from breakfast straight to the Sunninghill Hospital to show him and my mother the rings before going off for a night at a country hotel. Despite my father's condition and over our protestations, they insisted that they would throw us a wedding party, just as they had done for my brothers. A few weeks later, we invited a few people around to their home: although my father was very ill, he played the host with his trademark bonhomie and gave a characteristically well-wrought speech, brimming with love and cut with emotion. It was his last public act; he was back in hospital shortly afterwards and died three weeks later.

I write this now, from Paris, around the time of the first anniversary of our wedding and my father's death. C never takes his ring off; mine sits in a bowl on my desk amid the flotsam of a work-at-home life. I often fish it out and fiddle with it while I work, as I am doing right now; I screw it on and off, I flick it into goalposts made of books, I tap it against the teapot. I weigh it in my palm and am impressed, each time anew, with its heft. When I rub it, I conjure the empty rows of chairs at Mrs Austin's chapel on the day we were married and I fill them with family and friends, with characters fictional and historical, with all the people we might have invited to witness our union had we succumbed to one of the more conventional affairs that grace our respective families' photo albums.

My father is always there, at Edenvale, alongside my mother, as are C's parents, who died before I met him. So too are two older men, Edgar and Phil, whom I have interviewed several times during the past decade. It would be presumptuous to call these men fathers, or mentors, or even friends; we did not, for example, invite them to the farewell party we held shortly after our marriage and at which we revealed to our astonished friends that we had eloped. But such is the pleasure of an empty chapel: you can fill it retrospectively, endlessly, variously, and I often find Edgar and Phil there, sitting on those grey office chairs amid the ring boxes and the swans.*

II

Edgar had two wedding rings, he told me. He wore one on his left hand and the other around his neck.

The first was a solid gold signet, conjuring the respectability of a Soweto patriarch: his marriage of over fifty years; his decent clerical job; his home shared with his wife and fifteen of his progeny – children, grandchildren and great-grandchildren.

The second was a lush red silk tie, given to him by a male lover, since deceased. His family might have seen it as another item in his snappy wardrobe but he wore it with purpose, to commemorate the man. 'He worked for Liberty Life and he treated me so well. He was amazing! We would *go places*. It's still there, the tie. It's red, beautiful. *I love that tie!*' Edgar spoke with characteristic ebullience before anxiety overcame him: 'But at times it is painful when you have a friend who is not faithful . . .'

You could see the complexity of his situation wash across his

---

* At the request of both Phil and Edgar, all the names in this piece are pseudonyms. Certain biographical and contextual details have also been changed to protect confidentiality. Some of the material used here is from interviews conducted by Zethu Matebeni and Paul Mokgethi for Gay and Lesbian Memory in Action (GALA), Johannesburg.

broad, handsome features. He shimmered, in that way of some older people: there was a glint to his smile to go with the liver spots on his cheeks and the clouds in his eyes. 'You'd be sleeping next to your wife for six months and *you're* not having sex . . . I would advise anybody to honour their relationship and to be honest, because otherwise it kills you, spiritually and otherwise. Even at work your concentration is divided. In the life I have lived, you should have a room for disappointment.'

In my middle-class life I have always had a room: for sex, for love, for rest, for reading and writing, and – of course – for disappointment. Edgar had to make his rooms where he could find them.

Their wedding bands were the first things I noticed when I met Edgar and his friend Phil in 1998, at a Soweto tavern named Scotch's Place. While Edgar wore the conventional choice for a man of his generation and class, Phil's ring was groovy and geometric, with a sportif 'S' carved into the gold. Both rings were assertive and masculine, planed rather than curved, and spoke of the substance and solidity of their wearers. Phil, like Edgar, was a married grandfather; he owned a home in a middle-class part of Soweto and drove a car; he was approaching retirement from his own clerical job at a commercial company in town.

These were the days when a wedding ring still meant you were straight, or in the closet. And so Edgar and Phil's fingers flashed a particular code as the men sat in the semi-obscurity of Scotch's interior, having chosen a table that put them in the direct flight path between the doors to the yard and the bar. As patrons streamed in and out, Phil or Edgar would mutter something sotto voce, and a young man or two would linger for a moment, engage in conversation, and maybe sit down. By the time I left three hours later, chairs had been pulled up all around them and tables pulled together. All these young men had impossibly waspy waists with button-down shirts neatly tucked into smartly pressed jeans, or tank tops riding well above the navel: '*amaphophodlwana*', Edgar and Phil called them, using *isingqum-ngqum*, the township gay slang, derived from Zulu migrant labourers; 'small boys'. A friend later explained that in regular township slang, the word was used to describe a frisky young animal, a kid or a puppy.

I noticed, at Scotch's, that Edgar and Phil never went outside to the yard, where most of the *amaphophodlwana* gathered. This was not the 1970s, when you could more easily be an 'After-Nine': go to a tavern after work under the pretence of just having a drink, and allow your gayness to show 'after nine' once all the straight men had gone home to their families or were too drunk anyway to notice what was going on. No: this was the late 1990s. Same-sex marriage was still a decade off but the constitution had outlawed discrimination on the basis of sexual orientation, and a gay youth scene was budding in Soweto. Places like Scotch's were openly gay, literally: the yard gave way to the street, where patrons gathered around cars blaring music, as if at any township street bash.

'Look at them,' Phil said, with desire and disapproval. 'We were not as free as they are today. Today they are very free. Very showy. You can see them miles away. I won't go around with a boy in a skinny top and a belly button outside, no. No, no, no, no.'

Edgar and Phil themselves dressed with conservative style – sharp shoes, crisply ironed slacks, Pringle shirts, fine watches. Phil was diminutive and light-skinned, wiry and twinkly, with a neatly trimmed peppercorn beard and expressively creased crescent-shaped eyes that suggested traces of Khoisan – or 'Hottentot' – blood. He had a stammer that might have been exacerbated by age but was nonetheless full of gentle mischief and occasionally blunt lasciviousness, and had a quiet charisma that seemed to attract the clientele at Scotch's. He was known as 'Mr Soweto' in his circle, and always had a trail of young men after him. 'You and your beautiful-ugly face!' laughed Edgar.

Edgar himself was tall, dark and well built – 'a typical Zulu man', Phil riposted playfully, pinching him in the side. He had the easy, straightforward confidence of a matinee idol or the lay preacher that he was: his shirt collar was opened to a gold chain, and he was given to exuberant laughter and emphatic stress. The two men bantered gently with each other, their intimacy suggesting that they might be old and comfortable lovers, which is how many saw them, although neither used this term to describe the other. Their friend Roger – a white man who introduced them to me and who has known them both for forty years – believes that in another life, a free life, they might have made a home together.

At Scotch's, they disagreed about when and how they met: Edgar was sure it was at a neighbour's home, shortly after they had both married and become fathers in the late 1960s. Phil was equally certain that it had been in the early 1970s, after he had given Edgar a lift home from Lee's Place, another tavern where gay men would gather 'after nine'.

'We clicked immediately,' Edgar said, as Phil nodded affirmation. 'We started going to social functions together. *Fishing* was our thing!' The word was Edgar's own, idiosyncratic rather than subcultural, but it describes beautifully that part of their lives spent together, as men away from their wives and families, engaged in the pursuit of illicit, underground intimacy.

Phil later elaborated: 'We shared more than a friend [does], but not as lovers. We shared the problems in marriages and the problems with lovers. If you just have a sex partner, no problems. But if you have a *lover*, someone you're going to miss, someone you're going to die to be with, then you have problems. You make an appointment, he doesn't come. Next day, he doesn't come. You need to speak to someone. That's when you'd go to Edgar.'

'Or you'd come to Edgar because I had a *phophodlwana* you want,' Edgar responded.

'See what I told you,' Phil addressed himself to me. 'Typical Zulu man.'

'Yes,' Edgar shot back with affected pride – '*Typical Zulu Man*' – before launching into the story of how his life only started at the age of eight in rural Zululand, when he became old enough to begin cattle-herding: 'In between herding cows, we boys would go for a swim. And that's where I started appreciating boys – swimming in the Mvoti River!' At the river, Edgar engaged in what was known as *hlobongo*, the traditional Nguni practice of non-penetrative sex used to channel the libidinal energies of boys before marriage. Generally, you did it with girls, but it was perfectly acceptable to do it with boys too – particularly among Zulus, where the great King Shaka had encouraged the practice among his male soldiers. As Edgar put it: 'Men would just be on their own for a decade, in battlefields and what have you, and they would do this, and I tell you, it's a beautiful experience to have a man with you. Zulus do it professionally!'

He turned to his friend with the air of challenge. 'Am I not right, Phil?'

'You are right . . .'

'*Professionally!* Although they would deny it in the presence of other people . . .'

'You are not denying it tonight, my dear.'

In 1944, when Edgar was ten and the South African economy was booming due to the war, his father found a job in Johannesburg and moved his family up from Zululand. They settled in Pimville, the 'native settlement' south-west of Johannesburg that would become the germ of Soweto. The focus of Edgar's Pimville youth was the Klip River, which ran through the township: here he joined other boys in recreating their traditional age-mate groups after school. They prodded the few scrawny goats and cows about; they swam; they fought with sticks; and they found each other's thighs.

Like many Soweto women, Edgar's mother took in washing for white households in Johannesburg. And Edgar, like many Soweto sons, would be sent into town to collect the laundry and then drop it off when done. And so – as happens with boys all over the world when they discover trains and the cities they lead to – his life changed: having delivered the goods, he would go 'fishing' in Joubert

Park or at Park Station on his way back to the township. 'I was sixteen,' he had told me, 'a Zulu boy. Hefty! *Plumpy!* I wore shorts, very tight shorts! I was a fit young boy; men of all races would be attracted to me.'

Phil also grew up in Pimville; his father, a farm labourer, had come to town and found work during the wartime boom. Phil did not know Edgar as a boy – he went to the state high school rather than the mission school Edgar attended – but he also discovered his sexuality through washerwoman subterfuge. While still a schoolboy, he was working part-time at the fresh market on Saturdays. A customer, a young white man, struck up a conversation with him as he was carrying a sack of potatoes to the man's car. Having ascertained that Phil's mother took washing, the man proposed that she do some work for him – and that Phil collect it the following Tuesday afternoon. When he duly arrived, at a swish flat in Jeppe Street, he was greeted by a man with no clothes on. Phil let out a long, dramatic sigh as he relived the experience. '*Was-I-shocked!* I just looked, and looked. I had known there was something amiss with me, but I couldn't put a finger on it . . .' The man apologized for his nudity – all his underwear was in the laundry pile – and approached, tumescent, beseeching his visitor not to be afraid. 'Oh, I nearly fainted, and the next thing I knew, my trousers were pulled down . . . From that day I knew all along that I wanted a boy in my life. That was the thing I had wanted all along . . .'

Phil dropped out of school, much to the fury of his ambitious parents. 'I was too streetwise,' he explained to me. 'I liked the money. It was my chance of meeting men.' One of Phil's favourite haunts was the Union Grounds, at Joubert Park, where white soldiers were barracked after the war. 'He is on one side of the fence and you are on the other. He pulls down his pants, and puts his whatsisname through the fence, and you put your hands through the fence and get hold of him, and you do your thing. There and then. And he gives you two and sixpence.'

'Weren't you worried?' I asked.

'About what?'

'Being seen!'

'The lights in those days were not as bright as the lights today,' he deadpanned back.

Phil married for love. He met Mo on a train and fell for 'her beautiful country smile'. She was on the way to the city to finish her teacher training. He carried her luggage for her from the station to her lodgings and kept an eye on her once she was there. Their courtship was urban and sophisticated, even in apartheid Johannesburg. On their first date he took her to the movies at Sophiatown's famous Odin Cinema. This must have been in 1955, just months – or even weeks – before the bustling cosmopolitan district was demolished almost brick by brick and replaced by the white suburb of Triomf and its 65,000 inhabitants forcibly removed to Meadowlands, outside Soweto.

Such was Edgar's love of men, on the other hand, that he paid no attention to the possibility of marriage until his parents died in 1957. By this point he had 'fished' his way through vocational school in Soweto, where he had studied carpentry, and his Pimville church, where he had become a lay preacher. After his father's death he discovered that he would only be able to keep his meagre inheritance if he married. So he accepted the woman chosen for him by his relatives, and they quickly had a family; he gave up carpentry, and found the clerical job he would keep until retirement.

Now that Phil was married too, a neighbour found him work as a messenger in town. His wits were such that he was soon promoted to a desk job. It did not take him long to understand, as he put it to me, that 'you have to be rich to be gay', not least because you had to support two parallel lives. 'In married life you should be a responsible and trustworthy man,' he told me. 'That's why I'm still in the closet.'

Phil and Edgar held much stock in being exemplary family men: to provide, to be home for dinner, to be sober. Gay men, Edgar had it, were particularly good at this. 'The wife knows that you are responsible. She knows, at least, that you like to *improve the house!*' This cut them the slack they needed to lead their complicated lives.

They also experienced, alongside the pleasures of fatherhood, the often unutterable pain of raising children in South Africa in the latter half of the twentieth century. Neither man could bring himself to talk about the loss of his son: Edgar's to Aids and Phil's to the liberation struggle.

They never discussed their sexuality with their wives but Phil still cringes with humiliation when he recalls how he was once caught out. He had borrowed a book from a friend on homosexuality, and his wife came upon him reading it. He spluttered an excuse – it was just something he had picked up – and when the book went missing he assumed she must have thrown it away. Unbeknown to Phil, she had actually read the book, and loaned it to several of her girlfriends so that they might better understand their own marital circumstances. I know this from the book's owner, a younger black gay man, whom Mo once told: 'I know what he is. I can deal with it. He's a good man. And at least he is not running with other women. I'm not going to lose him.' Such are the tragic silences in marriages that she was not, ever, able to say this to Phil himself.

Phil was torn, he told me, 'between the love of my wife and the love of my "small boys". Gay life and straight life are different things. The comfort you get from a partner is different from the comfort you get from your wife. A partner is more intimate than a straight wife.' When I asked him to elaborate, his response was startlingly concrete: 'In the African tradition, sucking is taboo. Licking one's body, for a married woman, no. But with a gay boy, he can do whatever. He kisses you, he licks you, he sucks you, he does all the wonderful things. Once you have tasted a man, it's not easy to forget.'

The last time Phil and I met, it was shortly after the polygamous South African president, Jacob Zuma, had been forced to concede that he had had a baby – his twentieth child – as the result of an extramarital affair with a young Soweto woman. Phil disapproved strongly of Zuma but had some sympathy with his situation: older men needed younger partners, male or female, to keep the lifeblood – the bloodlines – coursing. Like their fathers, Phil and Edgar were patriarchs, with scant regard for the intimate needs of their women. They too were polygamists; unlike their fathers, though, their second 'wives' – their second lives – were secret.

Phil once said to me, about his life: 'To be black and gay, uh, uh, uh! It was double trouble.' He explained: 'Gay life in Johannesburg, it was very tough, especially among blacks because of the curfew, and your freedom and your privacy was the most important thing. With whites, I would say, it was much easier.'

The apartheid city was a place of manifest oppression. Even if they had lived there for two or three generations, black people were 'temporary sojourners' who had to leave by curfew if they were not barracked in servants' quarters. Very few black men went through life without a visit to 'Number Four', the dreaded Old Fort Prison, on a pass offence.

And yet the city was also a place of possibility and even, paradoxically, liberation. You could lose yourself in the crowd, away from the prying eyes and constraints of your community; you could spend your money on something other than beer – the only commodity widely available in the township. I will never forget the bitter-sweet story an older black man once told me, about how exciting it was to strut down Eloff Street, buying clothing by pointing at what you wanted from outside the shop window: black people, obviously, could not try on white clothes. Never mind: you returned home on Saturday afternoon to the smoggy township – Soweto was only electrified in the late 1970s – with the proof of your urbanity in hand and you felt a man of the world.

Once Edgar and Phil came to the city – first on the washerwoman pretext, and then because of their jobs – they found a new level of freedom. Or perhaps, more accurately, they learned how to play a new game of cunning, taking advantage of the opportunities now available to them while avoiding the double jeopardy of being black and being gay.

You might meet another black man in a desperate tussle in a locked toilet stall at Park Station or through a furtive grope on the crowded train home, but if you wanted a bit of space and a bit of time – if you actually wanted to undress and caress – you needed to find a white man. This was not so easy. A whole raft of laws prevented black people and white people from doing anything other than working together – and even then, only if blacks were in menial jobs. The Immorality Act proscribed sex across the colour bar, and in 1964 alone, 155 couples were convicted of this crime. And of course, in this time of intense political repression (Nelson Mandela was arrested in 1962 and sentenced to life imprisonment in the Rivonia Trial in 1964), any interaction across the colour bar could be interpreted as subversive activity and land you in jail.

All through the 1950s and early 1960s, there were periodic crackdowns on homosexual activity in Johannesburg, particularly at Joubert Park, the city's primary cruising ground. Both Edgar and Phil managed to avoid arrest but they know many men who did not. Phil recalls the humiliation visited upon two friends who were arrested in a sting – and were forced to shuffle along the pavement to the police van past commuters who could well have been their neighbours, with their pants around their ankles.

Once he was working in the city, Edgar found his way, during lunch hour, to Joubert Park. Here, he and other black men would linger on the post office steps waiting for white men to drive by and pick them up. This is how he met his first white lover. For five years, the man would collect him at lunchtime, take him to his flat in Malvern and get him back to work in time for the afternoon shift. 'I accepted it. If it's love, it's love at its best. If it's not, it's not. I've always lived that way.'

Sometimes, the white men would invite them back on the weekend, for a party; here they would meet other black men – also married, also from the township. 'You'd have to go through the tradesmen's entrance,' Phil told me, 'or you'd be introduced to the watchman as someone bringing the washing. Or you'd pretend to be helping your friend by carrying a heavy thing into his flat, or delivering a loaf of bread.'

In this way Phil and Edgar found themselves frequently, over the years, at the home of their friend Roger, the white man who initially introduced me to both of them. 'Our lives revolved around trying to get around the law, or beneath it,' Roger told me, as we sat in the suburban Johannesburg home he shared with his long-term partner, a black man named Sello who – extraordinarily – lived in white Johannesburg with him and worked as a professional from the mid-1970s onwards: his Botswana passport afforded him the reviled 'honourary white' status that enabled him to live in the city.

Roger is intense, verbal, pallid and precise; he is always dressed in the pastel colours – mauve tie against lemon shirt – of a Madison Avenue executive. A good decade younger than Phil, whom he had met in 1962 while a student at Wits University through the small mixed-race scene that had clustered around the post office steps and then found its way upstairs to the apartments of two older gay men, one Austrian and the other German. After a brief fling, Roger and Phil became lifelong friends; through Phil, he later met Edgar.

Roger's home is high up on one of the dramatic ridges north of the city, where he has transformed a rather ordinary 1930s bungalow into an Edwardian folly, with conservatories, statuaries and gazebos. He has also planted borders of soaring cypresses, entirely obstructing the home's magnificent view over Johannesburg. This was deliberate, Roger said: he needed to make a refuge for himself and Sello, and for their friends.

'Our intention was to make a welcoming atmosphere,' he told me as we sat in his living room looking down on the formal gardens beneath, set out around a sundial, 'a place where our black friends could meet us and each other safely and feel secure in the white part of town, particularly if it was after curfew.' There were certain rules:

the bath was always full, for example, so that you could wash off someone else's bodily fluids if there was a raid, and the music and chatter was always kept low, so as not to attract attention.

Edgar became uncharacteristically dreamy when he talked about Roger's garden. One might imagine how he felt, arriving there after having evaded his family-filled matchbox home, the incessant township noise, the sharp-elbowed train, the Eloff Street crush, the crime-filled streets, curfew gauntlets. 'Sometimes I would just go there by myself, even if I did not have a boy, just to sit in that Garden of Eden and chat to Roger.'

The reference to not having a boy stems from the usual nature of the gatherings at Roger's home and the homes of other white friends: they were about sex, and they were somewhat transactive. The white men would provide the space for their black friends and their partners to have sex freely and without shame or fear of disclosure; their black friends – Edgar and Phil, in particular – would trail a wake of *amaphophodlwana* to share with their hosts. It was never, however, explicitly about money and, it seems, neither side felt exploited.

Phil is emphatic, and characteristically straightforward about the benefits of lifelong friendship with Roger. As I sat with him, in March 2010, in his home – a solid-face brick suburban ranch house with a red-tiled roof that would not be out of place in a 'white' suburb like Randburg or Centurion – I asked him if being gay had opened up a broader world.

'Oh, yes,' he replied. 'Yes, yes, yes, yes. I got in touch and I got wiser. If I wasn't gay I wouldn't be staying in a house like this.'

Was he suggesting that his white friends had paid for it? Not at all: his employer had been an early facilitator of mortgages for black people, and he had been one of the first homeowners in Soweto, over fifty years ago. He explained himself, with a sweep of a hand that took in the leather couches, the flokati rugs, the books, the babbling Italianate water feature and fish pond, the modish patio furniture around it: 'This, all of this, I copied from the white friends I used to visit. Roger taught me a lot.' Phil and his wife were also, frequently,

Roger's guests at business functions; Roger's liberal younger colleagues would invite them home to their families, as a mark of their worldliness. 'So I would go to their homes, see all these beautiful things, and I would say, "One day, I'll have those things to myself. I'll have a house like this."'

One of the things Phil and Edgar shared, in contrast to their other black gay friends, was that neither was particularly interested in white men as sexual partners. Phil was blunt as ever about this: the only whites who were interested sexually in blacks were older men who could no longer attract young white men, and who thus sought 'to console themselves with young black men. Me, on the other hand, I have to have a younger man, or I do not get an erection. Even now, so long as he is younger, I will get hard. This is why black men are for me!'

Phil has had four lovers in his life, he says; all black men from Soweto. The first three broke his heart. The fourth has been with him for the past four years. His name is J.B., he is twenty-three years old, he lives with his family in one of the squatter camps surrounding the township, and he works as a security foreman.

There were a couple of rare, treasured places where, during the years of apartheid, Phil and Edgar could relax among other black people in the city. One was the Non-European Dining Room at Park Station, set up by the government in the early 1960s to show the world that blacks really were 'separate but equal'. It might have been an apartheid publicity exercise but it was also 'the only place in town' where black people were afforded the dignity of being able to 'sit down and have a drink, and eat a meal', Phil told me. Propaganda photographs show well-dressed black couples, or groups of businessmen, sitting at formally laid tables in an airy modernist interior of wood, light and geometric pattern, attended by liveried black waiters.

According to Phil and Edgar, most of these waiters were gay and a subculture quickly developed around them. Telling me this story,

Phil slid into another, about female prostitutes, who also frequented the restaurant. They would be picked up by white johns outside the station, and when they went back to their clients' homes they would make an arrangement with the manservant in the back room: if the house was raided, the working girl would rush into the 'boy's room' and climb into bed with him, pretending she was his girlfriend. She might be charged with contravening pass regulations but at least she would evade the far more severe Immorality Act.

The reason Phil was telling me this story became clear as he continued. It was a story about curfew and what you did if you missed the last train. Instead of running to the station, where the police would be waiting to pile all the laggards into their vans and haul them off to Number Four, you would make your way to Peter's place. Peter was a domestic worker who lived in a 'boy's room' behind his employer's house in posh Forest Town, just a couple of miles from the city centre, and from the way Phil tells it, you might indeed *plan* to miss the last train back to Soweto. 'You'd get there and, oh brother, those were the days! His room would be full, so full of young men afraid to be roaming the streets at night.' As was often the custom, Peter raised his bed on sandbags and bricks to protect him from dog-demons, 'and he would make a bedding all around him for everyone coming in. I remember one time it was so full that you couldn't open the door. I slept against the door but in the morning when I woke up I was next to the bed, maybe even *under* the bed, because those were the days, if you have got someone gay next to you, you'd enjoy yourself for all the dry months that you never had a gay person with you!'

I worked out with Phil that this experience would have taken place in 1966 – the same year a more infamous party in Forest Town was raided by the police on 21 January at 14 Wychwood Road, where nine men were arrested for 'masquerading as women' (a law passed initially to catch criminals in disguise, but used occasionally against drag queens). The headline in the *Rand Daily Mail* read '350 IN MASS SEX ORGY'; the raid provoked a massive public outcry, with the Minister of Justice stating during a parliamentary investigation that 'we should not allow ourselves to be deceived into thinking that we may casually dispose of this viper in our midst by regarding it as innocent fun'.

This was South Africa's Stonewall moment. The state then proposed legislation that would make it illegal to be homosexual, and a spirited defence by a 'Law Reform' movement grew within the gay community, its meticulous submissions to a parliamentary committee succeeding in tempering the legislation. Nonetheless, three amendments were finally made to the Immorality Act: the first was to raise the age of consent for male homosexual acts from sixteen to nineteen; the second was to outlaw dildoes (which, police reported, were the primary tools of the trade of lesbianism). The third was the infamous 'Men at a Party' clause, which criminalized any 'male person who commits with another male person at a party any act which is calculated to stimulate sexual passion or give sexual gratification'. Most absurd was the definition of a 'party': 'any occasion where more than two persons are present'. At the Wychwood bash, the only black people present were in the kitchen, but what was happening under the bricks at Peter's place was a party by any definition.

I grew up a few kilometres north of Forest Town and, as an adult, have lived close by. When I am in Johannesburg I drive through the suburb once or twice a day. Each time I do, I get goosebumps thinking of the atomized geography of my home town; of these two outlaw gatherings that happened contemporaneously in the same leafy old randlord suburb: one in the main house and one in the boy's room, each off-limits to the other.

In the 1970s, Phil befriended Charles, a man from Zululand who had left his wife and children back home to come work in the city. Like thousands of other migrant labourers, Charles rented a room in one of Johannesburg's single-sex hostels – Mzimhlophe, on the northern fringes of Soweto. Charles had met a white man and moved into his house in the suburbs; his room was thus available, and he sublet it to Phil.

For the first time, Phil and Edgar had their own space in the township. It was tiny, not more than two metres squared, with a single bed, a little table and a wardrobe, but 'it was a special place for us', Edgar told me. 'We called it "our flat". We would pay rent every month. It was exciting to have our own place.' The keys would be left in a safe place at the hostel and the men would make their way to the 'flat' individually, for an hour or for the night if they had a partner. On weekends, if they could both find a way of being away from their families, they would be in the flat together: the tone in Edgar's voice as he described this suggests nothing less than the bliss of newly-weds.

Most of Mzimhlophe consisted – like all single-sex migrant hostels – of communal dormitories, where workers were housed in subhuman conditions. But because Phil's friend Charles held a good job and had connections (the hostels were tightly controlled by indunas from Chief Mangosuthu Buthelezi's Inkatha Zulu nationalist movement), he had managed to secure a single room along a lane reserved for foremen and other senior workers. This lane, just to the left as you entered the sprawling compound, had been commandeered by gay men. Here Edgar and Phil could go about their business protected not only by a single-sex environment where many men took 'wives' but by the extreme alienation of the place. 'We were left alone,' Edgar told me. 'People in the hostel, they just drink for themselves. At the hostel you just live your own life. You are not curious about other people's lives. It was cool.'

Anti-apartheid social scientists and activists have conventionally viewed the single-sex hostels as prisons, where sexual behaviour was a pathological symptom of the economic system that produced the hostel in the first place: men had been forced off the land and away from their families to work as the 'black gold' of the South African economy. Certainly, the conditions in the hostels were degrading and often violent. And certainly, as in prisons, many of the younger, more vulnerable men were – and still are, on the mines – forced to become 'wives'. More recently, historians have begun to understand the homosexual relationships among migrant labourers as a form of resistance rather than oppression but this reading, too, is over-determined. Some men – like Charles, like Phil and Edgar – simply were homosexual, and found their space at places like Mzimhlophe.

When Phil and I spoke about the confounding legacy of the hostels, he told me the story of his sole visit to a mine hostel, where life was far more regulated than in township hostels like Mzimhlophe. He had been invited by a friend, George, whom he had met at Mzimhlophe, to attend a dance. When he got to the hostel with a group of friends, however, the induna at the door did not know of a George and would not admit him. Eventually, Phil managed to explain who George was and the induna exclaimed: 'Oh, you mean Margaret! James Bond's wife!' Phil was surprised to discover that George had transformed into a glamorous and buxom hostess; James Bond was the chief induna, and so Phil and his friends were made especially welcome. During the dance, Phil was particularly entranced by a beautiful young Shangaan girl who could not have been more than eighteen and who danced with seductive shyness. Phil wanted her immediately but she was not available, as she was mourning her husband who had died in a mine accident six weeks previously. At four o'clock, those on the evening shift had to change and go back to work, and the girl came back to say goodbye before going underground. 'I couldn't believe it,' Phil told me. 'It was a man in gumboots and a helmet and overalls. He was a man, now, going underground, to work, maybe to his death, in that furnace, with the heat and the noise. But he was just a little boy; that's what I knew from having seen the dance. How can you send a child like that into the earth?'

Edgar and Phil lost their room in the mid-1980s, during the township uprisings that eventually shook apartheid off South Africa even as they stole Phil's firstborn son. Mzimhlophe, like all hostels, was a stronghold of the anti-ANC Inkatha movement; the Zulu migrants who lived there would go on the rampage in Soweto against the township residents, generating much antipathy against the hostel, which became a fortified bastion. It was no longer safe to go there, so Edgar and Phil stayed away. When Charles tried to get the room back for them once things had settled down, he was told that it had been commandeered by another man who had paid the indunas protection money to keep it.

At roughly the same time, the parties in town, at places like Roger and Sello's home, stopped abruptly. Phil blames politics for this, too. 'In 1986 there was a lot of hatred instilled in black boys. We would try to get them to come to town but they were not interested in being with whites any more. And police were also suspicious when they saw a group of blacks in town: they would harass you.' Roger remembers being stopped, taking Phil and Edgar back to Soweto during one of the States of Emergency; he had to pretend that they had been waiters at a function and that he was driving them home after dark.

As apartheid collapsed and the new society began to form itself through the violent years between 1986 and 1994, gay life too began to change. As the inner city went 'grey', so too did the gay bars and clubs become mixed: Edgar loved the Skyline, Johannesburg's oldest gay bar on Pretoria Street in Hillbrow, which was rapidly becoming the centre of the city's black gay youth scene; Phil preferred the more mixed Champions, opposite Park Station, where he kept his own bottle of gin behind the bar and was feted as a village elder. You no longer needed to trawl the Park Station toilets or find your way to the white suburbs for sex. If you could pay the entry fee, you could go to sex clubs like Gotham City or, later, the Factory; once the anti-pornography laws started crumbling, you could slip into film booths at Adult World. Phil's friend Charles broke up with his white boyfriend in the mid-1990s but did not need to move back into Mzimhlophe: by this point, black people could rent flats or rooms in town.

Meanwhile, in Soweto itself, places like Scotch's opened, and a younger generation started to reject the 'After-Nine' identity. For one thing, the youth uprisings from 1976 onwards had constituted a generational revolution: young people were no longer bound to their families, or tradition, in the same way. As a black middle class began to grow, young black professionals got their own places, in Soweto itself or in formerly white suburbs, making the space that people like Roger had once provided. After he lost Mzimhlophe, Phil found a lover who had not married and who had his own place in Soweto. Perhaps because he had the space, Phil says he experienced real love – and heartache – for the first time with a man.

III

The first thing Phil noticed when he regained consciousness at Baragwanath Hospital in Soweto in May 2003, was that his wedding ring was missing. His wife explained to him that he had driven his car through the intersection on the Old Potch Road and crashed into a truck. He had been in a coma for several weeks. Phil assumed, as did everyone, that he had been robbed by a bystander, but it came to him, after a while, that there had been someone else in the car. It took him a full year to recollect, he told me, that the person who must have taken his ring was a young man he had just found at Scotch's Place, and that when the crash happened they were on their way to find a place to have sex.

To be found injured in a car crash with a boy you have just picked up would have been, of course, one of Phil's worst nightmares, and so once he remembered the circumstances he was deeply relieved. Phil holds it as a matter of pride that none of his scores of pickups had ever exposed him. But this implies a code of honour among 'After-Nines' and the men who go with them: they are a particular tribe, a particular clan, and they watch out for each other. The boy had violated this code, and the only time I felt Phil's anger flare during our time together was when he described how he had bumped into the boy two years later. 'I told him he would never amount to anything and would land up in jail. He is sitting there now. I have been proven correct.'

Phil told me this story in March 2010 as we were driving with his friend Charles through Soweto to the Maponya Mall to have lunch. The mall is famous for the sculpture of a huge, trumpeting bull elephant at its entrance, a clarion to the new black middle class; with shops selling high-end brands, it had been built by one of Soweto's pioneer entrepreneurs and is much touted as a symbol of the entry of the township into global consumer culture. It is also, I discovered as the three of us sashayed through its neon avenues checking out the rather dubious talent, a prime location for what Edgar, had he been with us, would have called 'fishing'. Positioning themselves on a terrace overlooking the entrance to the mall, Phil and Charles indulged in low-camp repartee, with much talk of *amagamane* (young pumpkins), *ama-pinchies* (peaches), *amacasiba* (thighs) and *isiphefu* (bums). Phil, in particular, complained bitterly about ageing, even after it was pointed out to him that he currently had a devoted young lover whom he seemed to have no trouble pleasing.

Charles was the man from whom Phil and Edgar had rented their room in Mzimhlophe; he was now in his mid-sixties, shy and handsome, with the distended ear lobes of a traditional Zulu man. He seemed to have replaced Edgar as Phil's special friend; the two men spoke every day and Charles visited him a couple of times a week. As we walked back to my car, Charles muttered something I could not understand, and Phil affected outrage, pinching him in the side as I had seen him pinch Edgar over a decade ago at Scotch's.

'What was that about?' I asked.

Phil translated what Charles had just said to him: 'I noticed you swinging your hips, and at first I thought you were doing it to attract the small boys. Then I realized it's only your limp from your accident.'

I had hoped that Edgar would join us at the Maponya Mall too, but he was not answering his cellphone. Phil told me his old friend was bedridden; he believed it was cancer and was annoyed with Edgar for refusing to consult Western doctors. 'That old Zulu has gone back to Zululand in his head!'

The two men barely ever saw each other any more. In recent years, they had been getting together once a month, when Edgar went to Baragwanath Hospital to collect his medication. Phil, who lived nearby, would drive over to meet him, bring him back to his house for tea, then take him home. But now Edgar was too ill to get to the hospital and Phil did not like to drive the distance, all the way across sprawling Soweto, to Edgar's home in Protea.

The last time I had seen Edgar had been in mid-2008, when I had asked him to participate in an exhibition I was curating, which told the story of Johannesburg through eight gay, lesbian and transsexual people. Although he was already ill and lame – he needed a wheelchair – he had agreed to take part, as long as we did not identify him in any way. For this reason, we used as his signature portrait a close-up photograph of his left hand, blown up into a four-metre-high banner; his wedding ring a flash of gold on the ashen parchment of his wrinkled hand.

We had arranged for a van to transport him to the museum, and I wheeled him into the auditorium for the opening event. I had not seen him for a few years and I was startled at the change: the only memory of his heft was to be found in the folds of skin hanging off his gangly frame. Still, he was sexy, an outrageous flirt, his face igniting every time a younger man paid him any attention. I introduced him to C and he approved. 'Very handsome and charming,' he told me, adding that despite much opportunity he had never been with an Indian man himself. When I mentioned our nuptial plans, he delightedly offered himself as the priest, and we chuckled a little about how we would spirit him out of his family home for the ceremony.

I watched Edgar intently as the South African Chief Justice, Pius Langa – a black man of his age – gave a keynote address underscoring the constitutional equality that gay people now had in South Africa. 'This is *wonderful!*' Edgar said to me afterwards, gesturing expansively at the crowd. 'Just seeing these young people makes me feel free even if it is too late for me.'

A week or so after our visit to the Maponya Mall, Phil decided to drive over to Protea, to check up on his old friend. When he arrived at the house, he learned that Edgar had died a few days previously, after a night in the hospital. The funeral had not yet taken place, however, and he was able to attend; there were only two other gay men present.

Phil called Roger to tell him about Edgar's death but when Roger tried to get information about the funeral Phil became vague and confused. Roger worried, he told me, that Phil might be developing memory problems. But it seemed to me that something else was going on. Phil would not even have known about the funeral had he not arrived unexpectedly at Edgar's home. He must have understood that his friend was being claimed back in death by family and clan and church, from the world of the After-Nines.

Phil's wife, Mo, died in 2008, after a lengthy and very debilitating illness. A year later, Phil told me about it as we sat in the living room of his house, a tray of mid-morning tea and biscuits between us, the sliding door closed against the prying eyes of the housekeeper bustling about the kitchen. If Mo had been alive, it would have been impossible to be in the house at all.

Phil had devoted himself, for several years, to looking after her, and he remembered her suffering with great sadness. Clearly her death had given him more space – his young lover J.B. now stayed over once or twice a month, for example – but he did not understand this as new freedom. Since Mo's death, 'a lot of whites who I have met have asked me: "Phil, why don't you come out into the open?" I say: "I've lived a lie for so long, I would hate to burst this balloon. I don't know what would happen. So I would rather take this with me, to the grave."'

J.B. had been with him through 'thick and thin', through Mo's illness and then the bereavement period, and Phil's family had come to accept the young man's presence. Still, as always, he had needed to dissemble: he told his children that J.B.'s father had been a work colleague who had died young and that he had made a death-bed pledge to look after the boy. 'You have to lead the life of a lie,' he told me. 'You have to tell lies and be careful you are not caught. That has been my life.'

As if on cue, Phil's sister arrived unexpectedly with a box of cabbages she had brought back from the countryside. While she was making her way across the lawn, Phil and I hurriedly agreed on a story to explain the unusual presence of a white visitor: I had come from England with a gift from my father, who had been Phil's boss many years previously. I received the sister's warm greetings – 'Welcome to Soweto! You are at home here!' – before Phil scuttled me out of the house.

Earlier, I had taken him into the garden to photograph his wedding ring, for an image I hoped to use alongside Edgar's. We had chatted playfully as he lured the winter sunlight on to his golden signet by shimmering his hand, and I told him about my own ring at home, on my desk in Paris.

'Gay marriage!' he exclaimed. 'Who would have believed? Edgar and I used to say, "Not in our lifetime . . ." It's like how we felt at the end of apartheid. You have to pinch yourself. It was a white wedding, I trust?'

I laughed. 'No, Home Affairs!'

'Which one?'

'Edenvale.'

He fired a round of incredulous clicks off the roof of his mouth before exhaling a laugh, or a cheer, that drew his skin tightly, in wrinkled folds, around dancing cornflower eyes. ■

Lukas Prize Project Awards 2011
Honoring the best in non-fiction

cʒ

$30,000 for a Work in Progress
$10,000 for the J. Anthony Lukas Non-Fiction Prize
$10,000 for the Mark Lynton History Prize

www.lukasprize.org

in conjunction with

 **Nieman Foundation**
for Journalism at Harvard   Columbia Journalism School ♜

GRANTA

LAST MAN IN TOWER

Aravind Adiga

He went back to bed. In the old days, his wife's tea and talk and perfume would wake him up. He closed his eyes.

Hai-ya! Hai-ya!

Screams from down below. The two sons of Ajwani, the broker, began the morning by practising tae kwon do in full uniform in their living room. Ajwani's boys were the athletic champions of the Society. The eldest, Ravi, had won a tremendous victory in the martial arts competition last year. As a gesture of the Society's gratitude, he was asked to dip his hand in kerosene and leave a memento of his victorious body on the front wall, where it could still be seen (or so everyone was sure), just above Mrs Saldanha's kitchen window.

Now from Masterji's left, a callisthenic voice, flipping diphthongs up and down. 'Oy, oy, oyoyoyoy, my Ramu – come here . . . Ay, ay. Turn that way my prince, oyoyoy . . .' What was Ramu going to take to school for lunch? Masterji wondered, yawning and turning to the side.

A noise from the kitchen. The very noise Purnima used to make when chopping onions. He tiptoed into the kitchen to catch a ghost, if one was there. An old calendar was tapping on the wall. It was Purnima's private calendar, illustrated with an image of the goddess Lakshmi tipping over a pot full of gold coins, with key dates circled and marked in her private shorthand. She had consulted it to the day she had been admitted to hospital (12 October; circled), so he had not removed it at the start of the year.

He would have to walk a bit today with his grandson; in anticipation, he wrapped a pink orthopaedic cloth tightly around his arthritic left knee before putting on his trousers. Back at the teak-wood table he picked up *The Soul's Passageway After Death*.

The bell rang. Bushy-haired, bearded, bespectacled Ibrahim Kudwa, the cybercafe owner from Flat 4/C, with dandruff sprinkled like spots of wisdom on the shoulders of his green kurta.

'Did you see the sign, Masterji?' Kudwa pointed to the window. 'In the hole they made outside. I changed the sign from "Inconvenience is in Progress, Work is Regretted" to the other way.' Kudwa slapped his forehead. 'Sorry, I changed it from "Work is in Progress, Inconvenience is Regretted" to the other way round. I thought you would like to know.'

'Very impressive,' Masterji said, and patted his beaming neighbour. In the kitchen, the old calendar began tapping on the wall again, and Masterji forgot to offer his visitor even a cup of tea.

By midday, he was at the Byculla Zoo, leading his grandson by the hand, from cage to cage. The two of them had seen a lioness, two black bears rolling about in fresh grass, an alligator in emerald water, elephants, hippos, cobras and pythons.

The boy had questions: What is the name of that animal in the water – Who is the tiger yawning at – Why are the birds yellow? Masterji enjoyed giving names to the animals, and added a humorous story to explain why each one left his native land and came to Mumbai. 'Do you think of your grandmother?' he asked the boy from time to time.

The two of them stopped in front of a rectangular cage with bars and a low tin roof; an animal moved from one end to the other. The idlers who had turned up to the zoo, even the lovers, stopped at the cage. A green tarpaulin on the roofing made a phosphorescent glow through which the dark animal came, jauntily, as if chuckling, its tongue hanging out, until it stood up on a red guano-stained stone bench and reared its head; it got down, turned, went to the other end of the cage and reared its head again before turning back. It was filthy – it was majestic: the grey fleece, the dark doglike grinning face, the powerful striped lower limbs. Men and women watched it. Perhaps this mongrel beast looked like one of those – half-politician and half-criminal – who ruled the city, vile and necessary.

'What is its name?'

Masterji could not say. The syllables were there, on the tip of his tongue. But when he tried to speak they moved the other way, as if magnetically repulsed. He shrugged.

At once the boy seemed frightened, as if his grandfather's power, which lay in naming these animals, had ended.

To cheer him up, Masterji bought him some peanuts (though his daughter-in-law had told him not to feed the boy), and they ate on the grass. Masterji thought he was in a happy time of his life. The battles were over; the heat and light were dimmed.

Before it is too late, he thought, running his fingers through his grandson's curly hair, I must tell this boy all that we have been through. His grandmother and I. Life in Bombay in the old days. War in 1965 with Pakistan. War in 1971. The day they killed Indira Gandhi. So much more.

'More peanuts?' he asked.

The boy shook his head, and looked at his grandfather hopefully.

Sonal, his daughter-in-law, was waiting at the gate. She smiled as he talked on their drive into the city. His son lived in Marine Lines, an apartment furnished by the insurance company he worked for. When they reached there, Sonal served Masterji tea and bad news: his son had just sent a text message. He would not be coming home until midnight. Busy day at the office. 'Why don't you wait?' she suggested. 'You can stay overnight. It's your own home, after all . . .'

'I'll wait,' he said.

'Do you think of her a lot, Masterji?' she asked.

'All the time.' The words just burst out of him. He tapped the arms of his chair. 'Gaurav will remember when his grandfather died, in 1991, and she went to Suratkal to perform the last rites with her brothers, who lived there. When she came back to Mumbai, she said nothing for days. Then she confessed. "They locked me up in a room and made me sign a paper." Her own brothers! They threatened her until she signed over her share of their father's property and gold to them.'

Even now the memory stopped his breath. He had gone to see a lawyer at once. Four hundred rupees as a retainer, paid in cash up front. Masterji had come home and talked it over with Purnima.

'"We'll never put them behind bars," I told her. "Is it worth spending the money?" She thought about it and said, "All right, let it drop." Sometimes I would look back on the incident and ask myself, should I have paid for that lawyer? But whenever I brought it up with her, she just did this –' he shrugged '– and said that thing. Her favourite saying. "Man is like a goat tied to a pole." Meaning, all of us have some free will but not too much. One shouldn't judge oneself harshly.'

'That is so beautiful. She was a wonderful woman.' Sonal got up. 'I have to check on my father.'

Her father, once a respected banker, now suffered from advanced Alzheimer's. He lived with his daughter and son-in-law and was fed, bathed and clothed by them. As Sonal slipped into an inner room, Masterji silently commended her filial devotion. So rare in an age like this. He tapped his knee and tried to remember the name of that striped animal in the cage.

Sonal came out of her father's room with a blue book, which she placed on the table.

'The boy doesn't read much; he plays cricket. It is better that you keep it, since you are fond of books.'

Masterji opened the blue book. The *Illustrated History of Science*. Purchased a decade ago at the Strand Book Shop in the city, maintained impeccably, until last week when he had given it to his grandson as a gift.

He got up from his chair. 'I'll go back now.'

'At this hour? The train will be packed.'

'What am I, a foreigner? I'll survive.'

'Are you sure you won't wait? Gaurav will be here . . .'

With his book in his hand, Masterji walked past the old buildings of Marine Lines, some of the oldest in the city – past porticos never penetrated by the sun and lit up at all times of day by yellow electric bulbs, stone eaves broken by saplings and placental mounds of sewage and dark earth piled up on wet roads. Along the Marine Lines train station he walked towards Churchgate.

He looked at the blue book in his hand. Was that flat so small they couldn't keep even one book of his in it? The boy's own grandfather – and they had to shove my gift back in my hands?

He opened the blue book and saw an illustration of Galileo.

'Hyena,' he said, and closed the book. That was the word he had not been able to find for Ronak.

'Hyena. My own daughter-in-law is a hyena to me.'

Don't think badly of her. He heard Purnima's voice. *It is your ugliest habit,* she had always warned him. *The way you get angry with people, crush them into cartoons, mock voices, manners, ideas; shrink flesh-and-blood humans into fireflies to hold in your palm.* She would cut his rage short by touching his brow (once holding a glass of ice-cold water to it) or by sending him out on an errand. Now who was there to control his anger?

He touched the *Illustrated History of Science* to his forehead and thought of her.

It was dark by the time he reached the Oval Maidan. The illuminated clock on the Rajabai tower, cloudy behind generations of grime and neglect, looked like a second moon, more articulate, speaking directly to men. He thought of his wife in this open space; he felt her calm here. Perhaps that calm was all he had ever had; behind it he had posed as a rational creature, a wise man for his pupils at St Catherine's and for his neighbours.

He did not want to go home. He did not want to lie down on that bed again.

He looked at the clock. After his wife's death, Mr Pinto came to him and said, 'You will eat with us from now on.' Three times a day he went down the stairs to sit at the Pintos' dining table, covered with a red-and-white chequerboard oilcloth they had brought back from Chicago. They did not have to announce that food was served. He heard the rattling of cutlery, the shaking of the chairs and, with the clairvoyance provided by hunger, he could look through his floorboards and see Mrs Pinto's maid Nina placing porcelain vessels filled with steaming prawn curry on the table. Raised as a strict vegetarian, Masterji had learned the taste of animals and fish in Bombay; exchanging his wife's lentil-and-vegetable regimen for the . Pintos' carnivorous diet was the only good thing, he said to himself, that had come of her death. The Pintos asked for nothing in return, but he came back every evening from the market with a fistful of coriander or ginger, which he deposited on their table. They would be delaying their dinner for him; he should find a payphone at once.

A loose page of the *Times of India* lay on the pavement. A student of his named Noronha wrote a column for the paper; for this reason he never stamped on it. He took a sudden sideways step to avoid the paper. The pavement began to slide away like sand. His left knee throbbed; things darkened. Spots twinkled in the darkness, like silica in a slab of granite. 'You're going to faint,' someone seemed to shout from afar, and he reached out to that voice for support; his hand alighted on something solid – a lamp post. He closed his eyes and concentrated on standing still.

Leaning against the lamp post. Breathing in and out. Now he heard the sound of wood being chopped from somewhere in the Oval Maidan. The blows of the axe came with metronomic regularity, like the hour hand on a grandfather clock: underneath them, he heard the crisp ticking of his own wristwatch, like little live splinters of seconds flying from the log. The two sounds quickened, as if in competition.

It was almost nine o'clock when he felt strong enough to continue home.

Churchgate train station: the shadows of the tall ceiling fans tremulous, like water lilies, as shoes tramped on them. It had been years since Masterji had taken the Western Line in rush hour. The train to Santa Cruz was just pulling in. He turned his face away as the women's compartments went past. Before the train stopped, passengers had begun jumping in, landing with thuds, nearly falling

over, recovering, scrambling for seats. Not an inch of free green
cushion by the time Masterji got in. Wait. In a corner, he did spot a
vacant patch of green but he was kept away by a man's hand – ah,
yes, he remembered now: the infamous evening-train 'card mafia'.
They were reserving a seat for a friend who always sat there to play
with them. Masterji held on to a pole for support. With one hand
he opened the blue book and turned the pages to find the section
on Galileo. The card mafia, their team complete, were now playing
their game, which would last them the hour and a quarter to Borivali
or Virar; their cards had, on the reverse side, the hands of a clock
at various angles, giving the impression of time passing with great
furiousness as they were dealt out. Marine Lines–Charni Road–
Grant Road–Mumbai Central–Elphinstone Road. Middle-aged
accountants, stockbrokers, insurance salesmen kept coming in at
each stop. Like an abdominal muscle, the human mass in the train
contracted. Masterji was squeezed: the *Illustrated History of Science*
progressively folded shut.

Now for the worst. The lights turned on in the train as it came
to a halt. Dadar station. Footfalls and pushing: in the dim first-class
compartment men multiplied like isotopes. A pot belly pressed
against Masterji – how hard a pot belly can feel! The smell of another's
shirt became the smell of his shirt. He remembered a line from his
college *Hamlet*. 'The *thousand* natural shocks that flesh is heir to'?
Shakespeare underestimated the trauma of life in Mumbai by a
big margin.

The pressure on him lessened. Through the barred windows of
the moving train he saw firecrackers exploding in the sky. Bodies
relaxed; faces glowed with the light from outside. Rockets shot out of
begrimed buildings. Was it a religious festival? Hindu, or Muslim, or
Parsi, or Jain, or Roman Catholic? Or something more mysterious: an
unplanned confluence of private euphoria – weddings, engagements,
birthdays, other incendiary celebrations in tandem.

At Bandra, he realized he had only one stop left, and began
pushing his way to the door. *I'm getting out too, old man. You should*

be patient. When the train stopped, he was three feet away from the door; he was pushed from behind and pushed those ahead of him. But now a counter-tide hit them all: men barged in from the platform. Those who wanted to get out at Santa Cruz wriggled, pressed, cursed, refused to give up, but the superior desperation of those wanting to get in won the day. The train moved; Masterji had missed his stop. 'Uncle, I'll make room for you.' One young man, who had seen his plight, moved back. 'Get out at Vile–Parle and take the next train up.' This time, when the train slowed, the mass of departing commuters shouted, in one voice, 'Move!' And nothing stopped them; they swept Masterji along with them on to the platform. Catching the Churchgate-bound train, he went back to Santa Cruz, where the station was so packed he had to climb the stairs that led out one step at a time.

He was released by the crowd into harsh light and strong fragrance. On the bridge that led out from the station, under bare electric bulbs, men sold orange and green perfumes in large bottles next to spreads of lemons, tennis shoes, key chains, wallets, *chikoos.* Cyclo-styled advertisements on yellow paper were handed to Masterji as he left the bridge.

He dropped the advertisements and walked down the stairs, avoiding the one-armed beggar, into a welcome-carpet of fructose. In the market by the station, mango sellers waited for the returning commuters: ripe and bursting, each mango was like a heartfelt apology from the city for the state of its trains. Masterji smelled the mangoes and accepted the apology. ■

THE B.O.G.
STANDARD

Philip Oltermann

The day we moved into our new English home in 1997, my father walked up to the living-room window and very slowly pushed open the lower ledge. *'Ein Sash Window – hast du so was schon mal gesehen?'* Had I ever seen anything like that? He let go of the brass handle. The ledge stayed in position, drawing an involuntary whistle from my father, followed by a grunt and a nod of the head. This acoustic code was well known in the family, a telltale sign that my father was admiring the robustness of a piece of furniture or machinery. The hung-sash window, my father explained, was a masterpiece of British craftsmanship: a complex pulley system of weights and counterweights elegantly hidden in the window frame, centuries old yet still state of the art. To him, the oblique charm of the sash window typified the appeal of our new home. It might have been small – smaller than the house my parents had been able to afford in Germany – but it made ingenious use of the little space it had, creating a Through-the-Looking-Glass effect, whereby the internal space was larger than what you expected from outside. We were charmed by our new English home, its nooks and crannies, its eccentric use of stairs and its damp bathroom carpets.

Like most northern Europeans, we were dedicated Anglophiles. Which is to say that we were practically half-English before we made the move: tea drinkers, shortbread nibblers, watchers of non-subtitled BBC comedies. When my father was offered a position at the London office of his company, it was a chance to complete the metamorphosis. My parents were ambitious: within weeks of our arrival, my father started demanding fried bacon and beans on toast for breakfast. My mother tried her hand at a Sunday roast. I was encouraged to take up cricket. But the road to Englishness wasn't always smooth. We soon discovered that the sash window had an irritating habit of rattling in the frame each time an aeroplane passed overhead (which was frequent – we lived on the Heathrow flight path). One or two of the windows didn't rattle – they had been painted shut, which was just as irritating. Cleaning a sash window proved to be difficult, if not impossible, because you couldn't reach the area where the two sheets of glass overlapped. After the summer, a neat rectangle of filth had crystallized in the middle of the two panes. When winter came, we had to move the sofas away from the windows to avoid the draught that sneaked through the gaps.

Other features we had originally admired began to grate. My mother's key snapped in the lock of our front door and several days were spent wondering why no one had thought of equipping the door with a handlebar, thus taking the pressure off the key on opening. There was an awkward encounter with a plumber who spent a week trying to fix a burst pipe before breaking down in tears and admitting that he didn't have a clue what he was doing.

There were constant roadworks outside our house: a patchwork of tarmac and cement which was ever-changing but never completed. '*Eine Arbeitsbeschaffungsmassnahme*,' my father said in a mouthful of Germanic compounds. A measure to keep people in work. No wonder England's unemployment figures were so low.

My parents still loved England, though now with a slightly desperate edge. Cans of bitter appeared in our fridge overnight. Bags of salt-and-vinegar crisps invaded the kitchen cupboard. One evening my father returned from work brandishing a fold-up roller scooter and declared to my mother's bewilderment that he would from now on make the journey to his office on two wheels. That was what English people did – they were eccentric!

But something wouldn't click into place. Our home, which we should have been familiar with by now, remained stubbornly strange. Nowhere was this as true as in our bathroom.

Using an English bathroom if you are used to German bathrooms was, I imagine, how it would feel to have been struck down by a severe nervous disease: the most basic things suddenly felt unfamiliar. There were never any light switches in English bathrooms, for example – even though they existed in the rest of the house. Instead, a piece of string dangled from the ceiling, occasionally with some wooden or ceramic ball attached, but often ending in a useless little knot. There were no power sockets, or if there were, they were made for strangely shaped plugs. English bathrooms, like English pubs, were also frequently carpeted – 'to keep your feet warm', a girlfriend later explained to me. A rectangular square was cut out from around the toilet, which in itself was fairly unremarkable, though its integrated flushing mechanism deserves a mention. It usually worked, though coaxing it into action, you needed the dedication and instinctive sense of rhythm usually required for starting the engine of a classic car. German flushes, in contrast, consisted of two buttons – one for big, one for small ('water saver') – and sprang into life with the mighty roar of a rocket launch. Either way, the toilet wasn't the real centrepiece of the English bathroom; the sink was. There were two taps: one for hot water and one for cold. The cold water was freezing; the hot water boiling. Right here was a puritan manifesto against the luxuries of modern living: the invention of the mixer tap had been stubbornly shunned. It took me years to internalize the hand-washing routine that I can now perform in my sleep – criss-crossing my soapy hands between the two jets of water while regulating the water pressure with my wrist. Back in those days I used to keep a little booklet with words and phrases I had picked up at school or on the bus home. Between the words 'acquiescence' and 'bugle', there was a hastily scribbled entry which read: 'bog standard: average quality, verging on poor'. I remember how much sense that word made to me at the time, for the standard of English bogs really was 'below par'.

One crystal-clear December morning, a year after we'd moved into our new home, something finally cracked, physically and metaphorically. I walked into our living room to find that the overnight frost had left an enormous fissure across the lower part of the previously revered sash window. Enough was enough, my father announced. We needed new windows: not any old bog-standard window, but a 'tilt-and-turn', German standard. At that point, I had a brainwave. Upon my suggestion, my father contacted a local window-fitting company owned by the father of one of the boys at my new school: Sam West, who wore dark skater shoes and smoked cigarettes behind the sports hall. Workmen turned up at our house, fitted new windows and left, but instead of becoming my new best friend, Sam started to ignore me at the bus stop. It was another two years before I found out why. After sash had given way to tilt-and-turn, my father had written a letter to Sam's dad. 'Thank you for replacing our windows. However, it has to be said: in Germany everything is much more efficient.'

In hindsight, this story sounds like the punchline to some stupid joke. Like the one about the German child who never says a word until one day its mother forgets to change the bedding. ('Mother, my bedclothes are dirty.' 'You can speak! But why didn't you say anything until now?' 'Because until now, Mother, everything has been satisfactory.') A few weeks at an English public school taught me pretty quickly that this is what Germans were meant to be like: humourless, efficient, robot-like.

What exactly was German efficiency? Was it being organized? I wasn't very good at being organized. Was it punctuality? I overslept on the day of my first AS exam. Or was it good workmanship: tilt-and-turn, Siemens, Miele, Vorsprung durch Technik? My father was undeniably German that way. For his PhD in engineering he had spent six years examining the viscosity of water as it approaches boiling point. This is important, he explained. As water turned into steam it expanded and as steam turned into water it contracted – nature was left playing catch-up. *Horror vacui*, nature's abhorrence of empty space, was key to understanding why matter could be animated. I usually glazed over at this point: nothing bored me more than engines.

My father was a genius at building and repairing things. We had a cellar in our old German home – *ein Bastelkeller* – from which he would emerge triumphantly every now and then, brandishing a newly repaired chair or a rewired toaster. I, on the other hand, was a complete and utter failure when it came to DIY. One afternoon my father and I went down to the *Bastelkeller* so that I could learn how to fix a puncture on my bike tyre. We emerged several hours later, the tyre still flat, my father's head hanging in despair, my own in shame.

M achines mattered to my father's generation. Born two years before the end of World War II, he had grown up in the decade of the so-called *Wirtschaftswunder*, when Marshall Plan money, the introduction of the Deutschmark and Ludwig Erhard's liberal market reforms enabled Germany to pass from post-war gloom to economic boom with miraculous speed. Nothing symbolized that rapid uplift in living standards more powerfully than the automobile. Between 1951 and 1961, the number of passenger cars in the country multiplied sevenfold; in 1953 Germany overtook Britain as Europe's leading car manufacturer. My father's first car was a Volkswagen Beetle, the most German of German machines. Like everything else in the country, it had an uncomfortable Nazi past (Hitler had sponsored the Volkswagen prototype, the 'Strength through Joy' car), yet its physical appearance was almost comically harmless. If American cars with their rocket-shaped headlights and their flamboyant wing mirrors seemed to imitate B-movie spaceships, the Beetle was akin to twentieth-century office stationery: less concerned with marking its space than making use of as little room as possible. Could a car with headlights that looked like frogs' eyes hurt anyone?

My parents bought their first Beetle for roughly double their joint monthly wages: 2,300 Deutschmarks. This was 1967, when my father was still an engineering student and shortly before my mother fell pregnant with my older brother, Ralf. There is a photograph of baby Ralf peering through the passenger-seat window on their first family holiday. It was taken in 1969, when my parents should really have been out on the streets protesting, or at least smoking weed in student communes. Instead, their life resembled one of those Volkswagen adverts of the time, in which young families zoomed into the sunburst sixties with big grins on their faces, using their new car as a sort of motorized picnic hamper. 'The big day . . . Finally a Volkswagen owner' was the kind of slogan they usually carried. The saving grace of the car in the photo is the fact that it has exactly the same eggshell colour as the Beetle you can see on the cover of the Beatles' *Abbey Road* album of the same year, strategically placed between a denim-clad George Harrison and barefoot Paul McCartney, a slightly obvious but forgivable visual gag: the fifth Beatle.

The British had their own equivalent of the 'people's car'. The Mini had a boxier shape than the Volkswagen, and its wheels were tiny; it looked as if an invisible hand was trying to pin it to the ground. Even more so than the Beetle, the Mini was a lifestyle symbol, inextricably tied up with music, art and fashion. Initial sales of the car were poor – at £300 it was pricey for flat-cap workers. Things only changed after the newly married Princess Margaret and her husband, Antony Armstrong-Jones, were spotted in a Mini which the car's Greek-born inventor, Alec Issigonis, had given them personally as a wedding present. The little car captured the imagination of an upwardly mobile nation. Marianne Faithfull was spotted driving a Mini to pick up Mick Jagger from rehab. Peter Sellers presented Britt Ekland with a Radford Mini de Ville GT for her birthday. Steve McQueen owned a Mini with chrome-plated wheels and a sunroof. Twiggy advertised a Mini wearing a mini. In 1969, the same year that the Beetle was featured on the cover of *Abbey Road*, Michael Caine drove a Mini Cooper down the steps of Turin's Gran Madre di Dio church in *The Italian Job*. Watching that movie now, you are struck by how the film's cool cocktail of music, fashion and slapstick comedy is interspersed with several nasty little digs at Britain's Continental neighbours, and Continental cars in particular. Most of the jokes are at the expense of the Italians: there is a deliciously prolonged shot of a red Lamborghini Miura crashing down a cliff within the first ten minutes of the film. In another scene the Minis race the Italian police on the roof of the Fiat factory. But a certain German car also gets a brief cameo. Seconds before the end of the famous opening sequence, thus easily missed, there is a glimpse of a Beetle stranded on the side of a mountain road.

In fact, the Beetle was a common object of ridicule in sixties Britain. At the beginning of the decade, Alec Issigonis had published a brochure called *A New Concept in Light Car Design*, in which he outlined the faults of 'that German motor'.

The weight distribution was all wrong, he explained. The vehicle was too heavy at the back and plagued by 'oversteer': a tendency to start swerving when the car takes corners at high speed. In addition, the gearbox was at the back of the car which made changing gears unnecessarily elaborate. There were two small luggage compartments – one big one, Issigonis thought, would have been more practical. The petrol tank was at the front, which increased the risk of fire in the case of a crash. Extra material was required for heating or ventilating the engine: depending on the weather, it was either boiling hot or freezing cold inside the car. On the other hand, in the Mini, the engine was fitted transversely at the front, sharing a space with the gearbox. The ten-inch tyres hardly protruded into the passenger cabin. Only 20 per cent of the car's inner space was taken up by machinery; making 80 per cent of the Mini inhabitable.

There's a great anecdote, according to which Alec Issigonis once went on a skiing holiday and got stuck at the bottom of a mountain, with no way of getting back up other than by being dragged by a Volkswagen Beetle. Issigonis complied, eventually, but not without screaming abuse at 'that German motor' all the way to the top. 'In Germany everything is much more efficient?' Not always, it seemed.

Several months after the episode with the cracked window, I sat down at my dad's computer and learned that the bog standard had nothing to do with toilets at all. It was in fact an acronym: B.O.G. standard, meaning 'British or German standard', a term that, linguists claimed, originated in the car industry during the 1960s and 70s and denoted a particularly high standard in engineering. I liked this. It hinted at an era of shared values and respectful appreciation, rather than the mutual mockery which seemed to dominate Anglo-German relations in the 1990s.

A few weeks later, by sheer coincidence, a friend took me to watch a Godard film at the National Film Theatre. *British Sounds*. Made in 1969, the film starts with a ten-minute tracking shot of men working on an assembly line inside a car factory, slowly cutting, welding and screwing an automobile into existence. In what might seem now almost a parody of agitprop cinema, the footage is overlaid with a male voice reading from Marx and Engels' *Communist Manifesto*: 'Masses of labourers loaded into factories and offices are organized like soldiers.' As it happens, the factory where Godard filmed this sequence is the BMC factory in Cowley, Oxfordshire, which was producing the Mini. The Cowley plant, as I later found out, was notorious for its disastrous working conditions. In 1969 alone there were 600 different strikes. Health and safety standards were practically non-existent: the lighting inside the factory was poor, the floor filthy with oil, the air heavy with lead dust. There was a glass roof which was occasionally removed in hot summer months. When the sun shone, you could see the lead glittering in the air. On their walk home, workers spat black phlegm on to the pavement.

Once, when the Cowley workers were invited on a tour of Volkswagen's Wolfsburg plant, they were shocked to find how different standards were in the German factory. The main hall was bright and clean. There was an open space in the centre of the factory where the entire workforce would assemble for general meetings. A third of the machinery used to build the German car was regularly taken out for overnight maintenance, substantially lowering the chances of faults and accidents. In Cowley, it took between fifteen and twenty men to equip the Mini with a door. In Wolfsburg, the Beetle was placed on a mechanical crucifix and turned on its side; the same stage of the car-making process required one operator. The Germans had become very good at putting together their poorly thought-out car, while the British had become very poor at putting their ingenious design into action.

Either way, it may be fair to say that the B.O.G. standard probably didn't merit the hopes and aspirations people had invested into British and German cars. In 1953 alone – as the economic boom was in full swing – 10,936 people died on German roads. When my father was a small boy, he was sitting on his grandfather's lap as their overladen Opel collided with an ambulance on a country road. He crashed through the windscreen but survived unscathed; his grandfather died. Years later my father's older brother was fatally injured when he lost control of his Ford on a tight corner. Another brother had died in a similarly tragic industrial accident at Hamburg's harbour. No one ever talked about it in our family, and I grew up knowing nothing about the two uncles I had never met. Only the two empty spaces next to my father's portrait on my grandmother's living-room cabinet hinted that something might be missing. It's as if Germans don't want to accept that even cars can sometimes let you down.

Rapid expansion followed by rapid extraction equals animation of matter: that is also the story of Germany and its economic miracle. And once you're moving, why stop and look back? By 1973 all major motoring countries in Europe had introduced upper speed limits – only West Germany didn't play by the rulebook. Even today you can zoom down the autobahn at full throttle; tribute to that very German blind faith in the perfection of machines. If the automobile fails – well, then we deserve to fail too.

By the time we moved to England, the 'B.O.G. standard' had lost all meaning. The Mini, for one, wasn't actually owned by a British company any more. Six years after Alec Issigonis's death in 1988, BMW, Germany's second-largest car maker after Volkswagen, bought the Rover Group, which owned the Mini. The British press feigned outrage at the deal because, for the first time in over ninety years, the country would be without a native mass-production car maker.

I wasn't all that surprised then, when I found out that the B.O.G. standard might never have existed in the first place. Flicking through the channels one evening, I chanced upon a panel quiz show in which the host elaborated that 'bog standard' was really a bastardization of the term 'box standard', a labelling format that was common among mass-produced toys such as the Meccano train set. In fact, continued the host, Meccano could be credited with not just one but two popular phrases. For discerning parents with disposable income, there was the train set in the 'box deluxe' edition, a phrase that later entered common parlance by spoonerist inversion as 'dox beluxe', or 'dog's bollocks'. Whether or not this is etymologically accurate doesn't matter – to me, it still rings true. By the time BMW bought the Mini, automobiles had long since lost the utopian glow they had for my parents' generation; for the boys at my English sixth-form college, cars were at best toys and at worst outlets for pent-up testosterone.

The marriage of BMW and Rover didn't last long. Even under BMW's directorship, Rover's factories continued to lose money – in part because the new management turned out to be anything but ruthlessly efficient and failed to implement the famed high standards of British engineering. In Germany, Rover became known variably as *der englische Patient* or 'the bottomless hole'. By the time I passed my A levels, Pischetsrieder had resigned and BMW had sold the majority of the Rover package back to a British investment company, keeping only the Mini.

My parents also pulled out of their British merger when my father retired. The house with the damp bathroom carpets and the retro-fitted tilt-and-turn was sold. A German van arrived empty and disappeared to the Continent loaded with furniture. I remained. I was the Mini in the deal, a mix-up of German and English spare parts, too far down the assembly line to be deconstructed. For the second year of my literature degree I moved into a student flat off the Cowley Road outside Oxford, a shabbier copy of my parental home, where paint peeled off the walls and soggy lino curled up on the kitchen floor. In 2001, a couple of miles from where I lived, BMW relaunched the Mini, though I was completely unaware of it, having by now cultivated a wilful ignorance of all things mechanical, as befitted a student of the loftier arts. I failed to notice that the B.O.G. standard had a happy ending after all, for the newly styled Mini managed to combine traditional British design with quality German engineering to achieve commercial success.

A few years later, on Christmas Eve, I went to my parents' new German home: an old red-brick house on the outskirts of Hamburg. Sometime between the traditional decorating of the Christmas tree in the afternoon and the unwrapping of presents in the evening, I wandered from room to room to inspect familiar features: the bulky front door with the solid metal handlebar, the tilt-and-turn windows and the smoothly tiled bathroom floor. I was about to run my hands over the chrome mixer tap when I saw out of the corner of my eye that my father was beckoning my three nephews, aged three to nine, to the cellar door. I silently followed them down the stairs. In the middle of the room where my parents stored wine, apple juice and old shoes, my father had set up a little table, covered in a blanket. He waited until his audience had come to a standstill. Then, with a theatrical flourish, he pulled away the cover to reveal a rusty old steam engine now gleaming under the bare light bulb like a fat little Buddha. Solemnly, my father lit a tealight underneath a small container and poured a few ounces of water into the opening. A minute later, a wheel started to turn, first slowly and then faster. A thin jet of steam escaped from a miniature chimney, and condensation dribbled from an exhaust at the other end.

My father turned to my nephews. 'Can someone explain to me how this works?'

Luis, aged six, thrust his hand in the air before my father had even finished his question. 'I can. You've put the water in at one end and it's coming out at the other.'

His brothers giggled. My father shook his head but smiled, while I realized that I would have struggled to explain it much better. The term *horror vacui* came to my mind, and I wondered if I should have tried earlier to understand what was going on inside the machine. ∎

Half-Mexican

Odd to be a half-Mexican, let me put it this way
I am Mexican + Mexican, then there's the question of the half
To say Mexican without the half, well it means another thing
One could say *only Mexican*
Then think of pyramids – obsidian flaw, flame etchings, goddesses with
Flayed visages claw feet & skulls as belts – these are not Mexican
They are existences, that is to say
Slavery, sinew, hearts shredded sacrifices for the continuum
Quarks & galaxies, the cosmic milk that flows into trees
Then darkness
                                What is the other – yes
It is Mexican too, yet it is formless, it is speckled with particles
European pieces? To say colony or power is incorrect
Better to think of Kant in his tiny room
Shuffling in his black socks seeking out the notion of time
Or Einstein re-working the erroneous equation
Concerning the way light bends – all this has to do with
The half, the half-thing when you are a half-being

Time
                Light

How they stalk you & how you beseech them
All this becomes your life-long project, that is
You are Mexican. One half Mexican the other half
Mexican, then the half against itself.

GRANTA

THEY ALWAYS COME IN THE NIGHT

Dinaw Mengestu

From the North Kivu capital of Goma, it takes an hour by helicopter to reach Walikale, a town in eastern Congo's largest and most troubled territory. With less than 2,000 miles of paved roads across the entire Democratic Republic, Walikale, like much of the North Kivu province it dominates, is virtually inaccessible by road, making frequent UN helicopter flights a necessity to resupply both the UN and Congolese troops stationed in the area. The view along the way is a montage of every image of equatorial beauty conceivable, from jagged volcanic tips to the neatly tended hillside farms that stretch for miles before giving way to a rolling, dense, green forest of trees through which an occasional stream or cluster of thatched-roof huts stands out.

Life for most villagers here consists of what profit they can glean from small trade, subsistence farming and the gruelling labour of the mineral mines for which the town is best known. But there is a natural abundance to the land that is evident to everyone; enough so that each conversation I have – with a soldier, with the owner of a small grocery store, with a group of teenage boys on the side of the road – includes both an acknowledgement of Walikale's vast riches and the price the territory has had to pay for them. That price informs the fierce scepticism behind each of these conversations, every one of which ends in a request for money, not out of the supplicant's greed or poverty, but out of the sense that I, like so many others, am profiting from their labour. This is a place as awash in natural wealth as it is in armed groups, from Rwandan rebels to domestic cadres, who, along with the Congolese military responsible for defeating them, have wreaked a collective havoc on a population living in what could be an Edenic corner of the earth.

The UN military base perched on Walikale's highest hill is a sprawling single-storey brick compound rumoured to have been the former home of a Belgian colonist. From there, the few hundred wooden homes and stores, the football field and the town centre seem to have been conjured out of a need to stake human claim to the ground. It is as if the town, when compared to the jungle that surrounds it, was built in defiance of the trees and towering bush that stand ready to reclaim the sprawling acres of cleared land on which it sits.

When I arrive, the town is tense with rumours that the Democratic Forces for the Liberation of Rwanda (FDLR), a Rwandan Hutu militia, are planning an attack during the upcoming celebrations to commemorate the Democratic Republic's fiftieth year of independence. But once I'm here, it's obvious how unlikely that is. Walikale is too heavily fortified by Congolese troops and the small but relatively well-armed UN team working with them. In reality, despite the symbolic appeal of striking Congolese soldiers on the anniversary of the nation's sovereignty, the FDLR no longer have the strength for such an attack. The militia's leadership, based in Germany, has recently been arrested and their numbers diminished by desertion and capture. Since losing territory during joint military operations between the Rwandan and Congolese governments, the FDLR have moved further west, away from the Rwandan border and the country they are reportedly fighting to regain. They are on the retreat, although to where exactly remains uncertain. After fleeing their homes and seventeen years of living, fighting and in some cases raising entire families in eastern Congo, this is an army of extended and deep rootlessness, an exile magnified to such a degree that it's almost impossible to understand what they're fighting for, or when and if they will ever stop. They are an army of the diaspora, from the leadership in Europe to the foot soldiers born in the refugee camps that have served as a steady recruiting source for the rebels.

My arrival at Walikale on the eve of the anniversary celebrations is partly due to the efforts of Caleb Kabanda, my Congolese fixer and translator. Caleb has a broad, wide face, punctuated by a seemingly permanent sceptical grin, notable for its missing top row of teeth. He has tracked the conflict, and the FDLR in particular, for years as a fixer and guide for journalists and celebrities, amassing a collection of hundreds of business cards and phone numbers of aid workers, Congolese politicians, soldiers, and the occasional rebel officer. He carries the cards with him at all times in a carefully sealed Ziploc bag, proof not only of his resourcefulness but of the sometimes extraordinary lengths to which he has gone in order to peel back yet another layer in a complicated conflict that has played out in the villages and towns he's known his entire life. He has proudly taken on the nickname Jack Bauer – homage to the hero of his favourite American television show. It's undeniably apt, given Caleb's military background and his insistence on finding the truth. If his constant exhortations that I discover and settle only for that truth feel more personal than professional, it's because they are.

It's Caleb's conviction that Walikale, at least at this particular moment, is the best chance we have of meeting active members of the FDLR, a task made exceedingly difficult by their recent retreat deep into the bush where they remain invisible, and by my own ethnic background. I had been warned repeatedly in Rwanda that I could easily be mistaken for a Tutsi, the same population nearly exterminated in that country's genocide by the founding commanders of the FDLR. The threat is real enough that the UN soldiers stationed in the town offer us armed patrols and a place to sleep on their base because if there's one tangible legacy that the rebels brought with them to the Congo, it's the racial ideology that helped shape the genocide. That ideology has, by and large, been erased, or at the very least deeply suppressed, in Rwanda, where no one is referred to any more as being Hutu or Tutsi. Even at the Mutobo demobilization camp for ex-FDLR members in northern Rwanda, where I spent several days before coming to the Congo, I felt only the briefest hint of that tension from a few of the more than 200 former rebels living there. Here, however, in eastern Congo, the strain remains fully intact, preserved and passed on in exile. I'm told to avoid certain parts of the country where the FDLR have blended in with the local population. On numerous occasions over the next two weeks I will find myself shocked and surprised at how easy it is to feel hunted.

The Congolese officials are determined to use the coming anniversary to celebrate the one institution – the army – that has undeniably failed the country through all fifty years of independence. But there is at least one group in Walikale that remains publicly opposed not only to the celebrations but also to the military's recent efforts to drive the FDLR out of the region. Sita Maud, a short and nearly bald, older man, is president of the town's civil-society collective. I meet him and his men in their headquarters – a modest brick building a few hundred feet away from the marching soldiers. As representatives of the town's civil institutions – from schools to local NGOs – this unofficial but well-organized committee airs the people's grievances and anger to whoever will listen. They are one of the groups Caleb insists I speak to if I 'really want to know the truth of what's happening'. According to Sita they will stay where they are tomorrow in what they claim to be protest but what could also just as easily be mistaken for helplessness.

'There will be no celebration for us tomorrow,' he says, and I can see that he stores a great deal of pride and meaning behind those words which, unlike everything else Sita says, are almost shouted. These are the only tools of protest he has, and he's determined to use them. The question he asks next is rhetorical but it bears both repeating and asking nonetheless: 'What do we have to celebrate?' Sita could just as easily have asked: 'What has this government or any government in fifty years of independence done for us?'

We discuss the government's most recent offensive against the FDLR. The portrait Sita paints of life in Walikale is disconcerting, not for its litany of abuse and violence at the hands of both government soldiers and the FDLR, but for the near-bottomless depths of frustration and the willingness with which he's prepared to express it: from the plundered villages hidden in the bush, the inhabitants brutalized and raped, to the corrupt soldiers who profit off the backs of the local miners.

'After the operations are over,' Sita says, 'they [the Congolese military] leave the people just like that – without support, without protection. It's because of the weakness of the government. When they liberate a place, they leave. The rebel groups come back. When the military is going on an operation to track the FDLR, afterwards *they* come back and loot the villages. Can you call that peace today?'

Since moving into the territory, the FDLR have subsisted by pillaging and forced labour. They have employed mass, systematic rape as a tactic of war, using sexual violence against the civilian population as a weapon of both terror and retribution intended as a deterrent or serving as punishment for co-operating with the UN and Congolese forces fighting them. They have done so with an impunity that makes a mockery of both the UN presence and the Congolese military. When I ask Sita if there have been any recent FDLR attacks in the area, he and his deputy list every village they can think of.

Mubi, Bilobio, Kalambo, Kabusa . . .

It is a list that covers only the better part of the current year, and one that fails to include the most recently ravaged village less than fifty kilometres from here. The FDLR's attacks are sporadic and occur throughout the region without warning; a viral presence, flaring from time to time in different locations across eastern Congo's heavily scarred body.

I ask Sita if the people have any trust left in the military, or if they believe there's any chance the army can bring peace. His response is appropriately cynical.

'How can we trust the soldiers?' He points to the sole window in the room, either towards the soldiers outside or to the jungle just behind them, as if to illustrate the close proximity between the two. 'The brother of one of the commanders is in the bush,' he says. That brother is a part of the Mai Mai, a general name for the many local armed militias that once served as communal self-defence forces but are today little more than poorly armed, self-interested rogue militias aligned with the FDLR.

For Sita, the difference between soldier and rebel is marginal, yet it exists, and ultimately it's the subtlety of that difference that frustrates him the most. It is in that divide that a nation like the Congo is made or broken. The soldiers in Walikale, both the UN and the Congolese – but most importantly the Congolese – are there to protect civilians, but no one believes that; neither the soldiers nor the civilian population around them. Once the troops marching outside Sita's office are in the bush, away from the tarmac road and the neatly demarcated white lines, away from the UN soldiers and the base that sustains them, with little money and even less food, there is not much chance that their recently polished shoes or the insignia of their rank will be enough to make them believe that they are any different from the FDLR. They will act precisely like the rebels they are chasing – ultimately, if the two share anything, it's that neither believes in the country they are supposedly fighting for.

Until his arrest in November 2009, the president of the FDLR was Ignace Murwanashyaka, a forty-seven-year-old refugee living in Mannheim, Germany. He had spent most of his adult life abroad, studying first in Sudan and later in Germany, where he completed his PhD in economics. The group's vice-president was another German-based expatriate, Straton Musoni; and its secretary, a former UN worker based in Paris who never faced prosecution for his role in the genocide. In an interview given from his home in Mannheim shortly before he was arrested, Murwanashyaka, dressed in a winter coat that made his already childish face seem even younger, compared himself to the president of a corporation.

Indeed, there is something corporate behind the FDLR's structure – a deliberate globalization and diffusion of risk that seems infinitely removed from the men in the bush. Unlike many rebel armies that have spread their terror across Africa in recent decades, the FDLR has remained organized after many years of combat. Even as the logic of their existence diminishes with each year in exile, their hierarchical structure remains, providing a semblance of stability that seems antithetical to the chaos they provoke. Part of that relative stability has come from having a political and military leadership based far away, with no ties to the genocide.

Murwanashyaka worked his way up the organization's ranks, rising to secretary for foreign affairs and eventually to president. In 2000, after marrying a German citizen and securing his visa, he underwent on-the-job military training in eastern Congo. Once back in Germany, he used his base and contacts in Western Europe to channel money to the FDLR, purchase weapons and, just as importantly, to rewrite the history of the militia from that of former genocidaires to liberation fighters opposed to what they referred to as the brutal regime of Rwandan president Paul Kagame. Murwanashyaka issued a series of press releases and, with a fellow expatriate, created a website for the FDLR. Occasionally, Murwanashyaka would visit a Hutu refugee camp and the rebels in the field. As for any visiting dignitary, parties were organized for the special guest from Germany. Beer, that most precious of commodities in camp life, would suddenly appear; dancers would dance and singers would sing.

The former FDLR soldiers who described Murwanashyaka's visits to me had all recently escaped the fighting and the FDLR commanders who promised them they would be killed if they ever tried. They are now worn, tired-looking middle-aged men living in Mutobo, the Rwandan rehabilitation camp created primarily for ex-FDLR combatants hoping to return home. That none of the soldiers at Mutobo who had met Murwanashyaka actually understood how this man – who had spent nearly all his adult life outside of Rwanda, and who now lived thousands of miles away in Europe – came to be their president, or how his decisions governed and shaped their lives, hardly mattered then, or even now.

At Mutobo, the genocide occupies an awkward, silent place, always present and yet rarely, if ever, spoken of directly. The official policy of the rehabilitation camps is not to discuss the genocide at all, and no one who enters Mutobo is questioned about where they may have been or what they might have done during those three pivotal months in which approximately 800,000 people were killed. That is to be left for another day, for the traditional *gacaca* courts where genocide crimes are confessed but not punished or, for more serious offences, the criminal courts that are still working their way through cases from that period. Mutobo is there strictly to open Rwanda's arms to its lost children, even if those children are men with a history of violence who have flecks of grey in their beards.

Jean Sayinzoga, the head of Rwanda's demobilization programme, is the embodiment of that open-arms philosophy. I think of Sayinzoga as the exact face the Rwandan government would like the world to think of when they consider the country. A tall, lanky, casually dressed and yet dignified man, Sayinzoga was an officer in the Rwanda Patriotic Army that brought the genocide to an end. Today he serves his country as a loyal government official, able to sing the praises of the ordered and civil post-genocide Rwanda from behind a desk in a sparsely furnished office. Like many Tutsi, his entire family was massacred in 1994, and yet he is the first to proclaim that he bears no grudge, holds no ill will towards those who did the killing. When I press Sayinzoga on whether that means even the genocidaires leading the FDLR are welcome in his camp, he doesn't hesitate before declaring: 'Yes, even those who killed.'

Walking around Camp Mutobo, which sits on Rwanda's far western edge, less than a hundred miles from the Congolese border in a landscape of mist-filled hills famous for their mountain gorillas, I'm continually surprised at the bored, languid air of the 220 men there – some of whom escaped from the FDLR only days before. They sit lazily on the grass, spread out in solitary heaps or clustered together, in wading boots and worn clothes, half asleep while a pair of massive, elderly cows graze nearby. I think, if we were only 200 kilometres away from here, in a village, or in the bush, there's a decent chance that I wouldn't walk away from many of you alive; yet

here, where there are no guards and no walls, the most I can muster
from you is a few quizzical stares and questions behind my back as
to what my origins really are.

After talking with soldiers at Mutobo, I'm convinced that most
of them played at best only a minor role in their own absorption
into the FDLR's ranks. All these men share a near-total absence of
purpose when it comes to their years spent in the bush. Most were
students when the genocide began, a few were tradesmen, and
some were only children. Munjore Eugene worked in a shoe factory.
On a slow walk around the camp, he describes to me how at twenty
he fled Kigali for eastern Congo, just before the city fell. I ask what
he did during the genocide to make him flee, and a nervous smile
breaks out over his face. 'Nothing,' he says. When I ask him again
in slightly more delicate terms, his grin grows wider, making him
even more enigmatic: a charming, gentle puzzle of a man. 'If I did
something,' he adds, 'I would tell you.' I hear a dozen variations of
that in the camp, and in some cases perhaps it's true. However, for
those who came from villages and districts where the extermination
of the Tutsi population was almost entire, we now know that it took
every able man in a village to complete the task. Their claims of
innocence, and the fact that at Mutobo they remain unchallenged,
are a part of the wilful amnesia much of the country is going through
in order to rebuild itself.

When it comes to Eugene's time with the FDLR, however, there
seems to be nothing he won't tell me. In the Hutu refugee camps in
eastern Congo he was a small-time trader, profiting from the massive,
irresponsible influx of aid that fed and armed the refugees. When
Congo's long-time dictator Mobutu Sese Seko was overthrown in
1996, the entire region broke out into war and Eugene fled again for
Brazzaville with other Rwandan refugees. It was there that he was
recruited into the army of Sassou-Nguesso (the current president
of the Republic of the Congo who was fighting for control over the
oil-rich country). When that war was over, FDLR leaders, with the
support of the Congolese government in Kinshasa, brought him

and hundreds of other Rwandan soldiers to the capital where they were provided with military training to help ward off an attack from Rwanda.

One of the child soldiers I had spoken to earlier told a similar story. He too had fought in Congo-Brazzaville, and in Angola and the Democratic Republic. At the time I had found it remarkable that someone so young could have been a part of so many different conflicts. His story seemed to strain credibility, until I heard Eugene's. Eugene had effectively fought in three different wars, on behalf of three different nations, virtually non-stop for fourteen years, primarily under the banner of the FDLR. Now that he was in Mutobo none of that seemed to matter, though, and it took very little to imagine someone like Eugene, handsome and still young, with an easy, natural charm, walking casually down the clean, ordered streets of Kigali, on his way to work or to one of the city's terraced cafes. There was nothing about him, or any of the other men at Mutobo, that pointed to the fact that until just a few days or weeks ago they were the killers in the bush whom I had been told to fear. It didn't take much for Eugene to leave that behind. That other Eugene had been formed and shaped by the emptiness of refugee life and the needs of the FDLR. They, along with men in Brazzaville and Kinshasa, had promised him that if he became a soldier he could return home someday. Now that he was in Rwanda, of his own free will, safe and secure with no threat of violence or punishment hovering over him, it was as if that other Eugene had never existed.

On the morning of Walikale's fiftieth anniversary celebrations I call on Colonel Chuma, an officer in the Congolese army and a friend of my translator, Caleb. Chuma, according to Caleb, is a speaker of the truth. He and his men are boarded up at the Life Hotel – a dilapidated two-storey wooden building with a large dusty courtyard and wrap-around balcony. Chuma and his men are here to take part in the military portion of that afternoon's parade to ensure the town's security. As commander of the second zone of operation, Chuma is effectively in charge of all the Congolese soldiers in the region. The day before, Chuma and a UN colonel had flown a reconnaissance mission over the village in search of possible FDLR combatants, a gesture intended to signify to the villagers watching from the football field that the government and the UN were on top of the situation. Chuma is short and muscular, with a bulldog ferocity that is magnified by his thin moustache and the silver pistol tucked into the back of his trousers. He leads us up to the balcony where two soldiers scramble to set up a table and chairs. From there we have a clear view over the hotel courtyard, where the rest of Chuma's soldiers sit in the shade, looking up.

Colonel Chuma is a gentleman from the beginning, delighted to play the role of host to his foreign guest. He runs over the history of his long military career, from rebel, to soldier, to rebel one last time, before returning to the government he now works for. He assures me that he takes the security of Walikale personally, and that his presence here in town is proof of his commitment. I believe him when he says that, because for all his bulldog fierceness, he also wants empathy, to be seen as one of the good guys in a country where most men in uniform want to be feared. He has the savvyness of someone who's given interviews before and therefore knows that much of what has been written about his army, particularly in recent months, has been damning. Without asking for it, he offers a confession, an apology and explanation for the state of the Congolese military.

'You know our army is still too young,' he says. 'We're trying to find ourselves. They come from everywhere in the country, from different rebel groups. We are in the course of reconstructing the army. It's true we come from the war. Our army is not like the army in the US, France, UK, Germany.'

It's at that moment that I trust him most. There is something warm, paternal almost, in Chuma's description of his soldiers. He talks about the army's new zero-tolerance policy and the harsh prison sentences that come with it for soldiers who loot, steal, pillage or rape, and that ferocity returns to his voice. He talks about the final victory over the FDLR, and lists the casualty figures from the most recent battle.

'We killed fifty-three FDLR. We recovered forty-three weapons,' he says.

And while the numbers themselves aren't telling of anything, the confidence that Chuma exudes when he talks about the most recent rout of the local FDLR makes the numbers seem as if they are somehow proof of his claim that it's only a matter of time now before the FDLR are defeated.

Briefly, the colonel succeeds in making a believer out of me.

When he says that if it weren't for the support of FDLR members in Europe they would have been defeated already, I say yes.

When he says that the FDLR are weak, and all the recent problems in eastern Congo began with them, I say yes.

When he says: 'We are determined to overcome all the obstacles to one day restore our country, to aspire to peace,' and that, 'The Congo needs its generals and colonels,' especially the ones like him, I say yes again. I want to believe that such statements, however mundane, are true, and I'm convinced that the colonel, and even Caleb, want to believe the same.

Before leaving for the parade, I ask Colonel Chuma what he knows about Musimiya, a tiny village an hour's drive away from where we are. The village was attacked a few days earlier by the FDLR and Mai Mai in a classic late-night hit-and-run attack that has become a hallmark of the group, and which left several Congolese soldiers and one infant badly wounded. For the first time during our interview Chuma finds it difficult to come up with an appropriate answer. He takes on a deliberate air of pensiveness as if trying to remember where he heard that name before.

'You mean Muji?' he asks, referring to a large, prosperous village in the opposite direction.

'No. Musimiya.'

He pauses for a moment longer, long enough for me to be certain that he's lying to me, and that he will continue to do so because there's no room for a place like Musimiya in the story he has just sold me.

'Ah, yes. Musimiya,' he finally says. 'It's very far away, not even in Walikali territory any more.' And while yes, he admits, there may have been some problem there, it would be 'better to go to Muji'. There, he promises me, we can interview as many of his soldiers as we like, and there we'll find the truth.

The long parade down Walikale town's newly painted road begins less than an hour after I've left the colonel. The first half of the parade is entirely given over to the military. Soldiers take turns marching and turning in unison while the national anthem is slowly torn apart by a military orchestra. A man dressed in full riot gear, with body armour and helmet, waddles down the road in the sweltering heat as if he were an apparition of Congo's future military might. Most of the villagers can hardly see what's happening; they're packed three rows deep on the side of the narrow road, and there they will remain for the next half-hour, bored but not listless in the heat, as everyone waits for the arrival of the territory's civil administrator, their highest ranking government official. When he arrives amid a small fanfare, dressed all in white with a blue sash across his barrel chest, he takes a turn marching down the street, granting his nod of approval to the soldiers and officers before sitting on a worn couch set up under a tent just for him. There is something monstrous about the whole affair that ends only when Walikale's civic groups take over the show. It's a remarkable display. For the next hour, seemingly every conceivable human alliance takes centre stage – the club for twins, the club for veterans, women who sing, women who sew, the karate club, and the multiple clubs for children and teenagers; all of them, dressed beautifully, take turns emerging from the line to claim their place in the celebrations and in the town that has rightfully always been theirs.

We know we've reached Musimiya when we see the charred remains of what was once a military outpost where the solitary blackened sticks left standing appear to be rising out of the ground as if that were the way nature had made them.

The soldiers who were here the night the FDLR attacked are still around, huddled together in the guard's post, the sole structure left intact. They are dressed in thin, sleeveless T-shirts, shorts and sandals. They have no weapons in sight, nothing to indicate that they could protect themselves, much less the village, if the FDLR were to return. They seem to be acutely aware of the irony of their situation. While they sit here unarmed, still within walking distance of the rebels who attacked them, a hundred other soldiers with weapons have finished marching in a parade and are sitting down with their first lukewarm beer of the afternoon. Lieutenant Gamuh, who has a wide unshaven face fixed into what I imagine to be a permanent scowl, is the officer in charge. There is something lazy and weary behind his movements and even his speech as he strains to maintain an air of control and formality while he interrogates Caleb about our reasons for being here. He grants us permission to ask him, and only him, questions with a slow nod of his head.

On the evening the FDLR attacked, he tells us, a storm moved in. It was just after 10 p.m. and all the soldiers, their families and most of the village had gone to sleep. Out of that darkness, just as it started to rain, twenty or thirty rebels crept from the jungle behind the outpost and began to open fire.

Gamuh admits, without any shame or embarrassment, that it was never really much of a fight. The FDLR had them outnumbered and benefited from the element of surprise. The soldiers stationed there had their wives and in some cases children with them, making it impossible for them to fight back without further risking the lives of their families. In the quick exchange of gunfire, one of those children – a one-month-old baby, was shot through the leg. What else could the soldiers do then but run for their lives, for the lives of their families? Gamuh never says it directly, but there's the obvious subtext: who would risk their lives and the lives of their family for an army that pays so little and asks so much?

As the soldiers fled into the jungle, they could see their camp

THEY ALWAYS COME IN THE NIGHT

burning and undoubtedly hear the screams from the second attack being launched on the village. I doubt any one of them even thought of going back.

When Gamuh finishes describing what happened that night, he tries hard to counter that defeat by offering his own assessment of the war. The FDLR are weak, that's why they have to hide in the bush. It's only a matter of time before they are defeated. He talks in slow, steady bursts of FARDC (the Armed Forces of the Democratic Republic) victories, with his hands folded over his knees, and an almost convincing arrogance, as if the most recent attack were a mere fluke and therefore almost irrelevant. Colonel Chuma, if he were here, would be proud.

As Gamuh speaks, one of his soldiers keeps trying to interrupt. The lieutenant ignores him, at which point the soldier turns to Caleb and addresses him directly. This goes on repeatedly for several minutes, and it's only once we've left the soldiers behind and are on our way into the village that Caleb tells me what the soldier was saying.

'He says: "Tell them the truth. Tell them we are out here dying."'

What Gamuh and Chuma won't admit to, at least not out loud or to anyone other than themselves, the villagers of Musimiya will cry out to anyone willing to listen. They are dying slow, quiet deaths of deprivation and fear, the kind of deaths that are most likely to go unnoticed because they occur not in a single day, but in stages that gradually take their toll on the will to marshal on and survive. As soon as we arrive in Musimiya, the men begin to gather around us. The procession is almost funereal in its silence. We're led into a one-room hut with the village chief, the elementary school principal and Zalirwa Nakaluka, the owner of what had been the only dry-goods store. Within a few minutes the room is completely full, as more men and boys crowd into the doorway and crouch on the floor, leaving little more than a thin sliver of light sneaking in. Everyone is there to hear Zalirwa's story. When

DINAW MENGESTU

the FDLR attacked five days ago they took the entire contents of his coffin-sized store, leaving only rows of empty, broken shelves that make it hard to imagine anything had ever been there to begin with. When they finished looting they took Zalirwa, forcing him to march with them barefoot into the jungle for two days with goods loaded on to his back.

Zalirwa describes what happened to him in a voice that barely rises above a whisper. He is a skinny, narrow man, full of sharp angles, from his long pointed chin on down. He gestures at his still-bare feet so I can see how swollen they are, and indeed they appear to have nearly doubled in size.

'For two days we were only walking,' he says. 'When I was tired they beat me with sticks. I was thinking this is my end. I am going to die.'

Instead Zalirwa eventually fell so far behind that there was a sizeable gap between the front and rear groups. Once it was dark, he used that distance to hide in the forest where he remained until he was certain that everyone had passed and he could begin finding his way back home. What he wants most now is to leave.

'If someone were to give me some money,' he said, 'I could go to Bukavu [the capital of the relatively stable South Kivu province], but I have nothing left.' He has no qualms claiming ownership of his destitution. If it's possible for an entire body to sulk, his does so. I am the closest thing to an aid agency that he has right now, and as much as possible, he wants me to know that. He wants only one thing, he tells me repeatedly, and that is to get out of here.

This was the fifth time in less than a year that Musimiya had been pillaged. The school principal, Nsesi Pilipili, lists the dates. 'It's always the same,' he says. 'They always come in the night.'
October 2009.
November 2009.
5 December 2009.
4 January 2010.

In the beginning a clear pattern emerged. A UN patrol would stop in the town to ask questions and shortly afterwards the FDLR would come down from their hiding places and exact revenge for the town's co-operation with the UN. More recently, however, there has been no pattern. The FDLR has been free to pillage at will, and Musimiya has become their designated whipping post. This last attack, which lasted for hours as the rebels went door to door, grabbing livestock, food, clothes, anything that might be of marginal use to them, speaks as much of the town's vulnerability as it does of the rebels' utter lack of fear.

'Better to leave us dead,' Nsesi says. 'Look at how we're dressed.' He points to a young boy wearing what is clearly a woman's dress half-tucked into trousers that are far too big. He points to the village chief, dressed in oversized rags. 'How can you live, getting pillaged, *pillaged*? When I came back I saw my home looted. School destroyed. We are like abandoned people. How come there is no one that talks about our village?'

I assure them, as best I can, that I will talk about their village. I will say it exists, even if it can't be found on a map. The lengths to which such minor reassurances go are heartbreaking, and I can feel mine doing so as I speak. The men in the room, most of whom have hardly moved or spoken, thank me, even though I have nothing to offer them other than a vague and difficult-to-imagine proof that someday, someone else out there in the world will know about them, and that they will not have been forgotten.

At some point while driving further north into Rutshuru territory in search of an FDLR captain who has said he would consider meeting for an interview, a slight but palatable change occurs. There's a tension different in shape and context from what I had felt in Walikale or Rwanda, and Caleb is aware of it as well. I had felt fleeting moments of it the previous day in the refugee camp built outside the UN headquarters where hundreds of Congolese, mainly Hutu displaced from the fighting, had been living. There was a menacing edge in the looks directed towards me that was new, but now I had a greater sense of being on the outside, of having crossed into a landscape where my very presence felt intrusive.

Unlike Walikale, the villages and towns here are large and populated with small hotels, stores and restaurants; they have a sizeable military presence. I had spoken earlier with a soldier, who had recently been shot in the leg by the FDLR, about the group's pervasive presence in the region. He claimed that it was only because the villages were aiding the rebels that they persisted, and that was why his patrol was ambushed in broad daylight. It's hard to see how the FDLR were able to ambush a patrol in the middle of the day – but then I realize it's not really much of an ambush if they are there all the time. Until recently, such an attack would have been difficult to imagine because there would have been no reason for it to occur. The Congolese troops stationed in the area were sociable, even amicable, with the FDLR. I had been told in Mutobo by many of the former rebels that when they needed new weapons or bullets, they often bought them from the Congolese soldiers – and of course it was in places like Rutshuru, where enemy lines are continually drawn and redrawn, that such trade could occur.

We finally stop in Nyanzala, a town known for its close relationship with the FDLR. It's only one village away from where the captain we're hoping to speak to lives. Caleb and I set out on foot through the town. In another village, in other times, in other countries, with someone like Caleb with me, I could easily spend the better part of a day walking through a town like this, talking to whomever came our way, but we both know that's impossible from the moment we step outside the car. After a few minutes of intense stares, Caleb guides us into a small dry-goods store, one that is almost exactly the same in shape and size as that of Zalirwa in Walikale, and that I imagine holds similar stock.

We buy a few bottles of water and while pretending to survey our next purchase, Caleb asks the shopkeeper if he could answer a few questions for us. He looks to be no older than thirty, the man behind the counter. I know nothing about him, and neither does Caleb. What Caleb does know for certain is that when it comes to the FDLR and the violence that surrounds them, the young man will have something to say. It will be the truth, inasmuch as it is lived and experienced within the confines of one man's life behind a dry-goods counter. That truth will resonate precisely within the limits of the roughly eight-by-seven-feet dimensions of the store's walls. Some of it may seep out further into the village, where parts of it are generally agreed upon and taken for granted. According to the man, who refuses to give his name, the problem in Nyanzala isn't the FDLR, but the army.

'An army brigade and the FDLR were living here together,' he says. 'Then they brought a more integrated brigade. They are the ones who loot and rape.'

As he talks he steps further back, leaning against the wall as if searching for more space to retreat into. I ask him what he thinks will happen next; who, if anyone, will win.

'The FARDC, they don't have the strength to keep fighting,' he says. 'They attack then come back. The FDLR, they stay in the field. You can meet them there and they don't do anything against you. They don't trouble the population.'

And while there is ample proof to contradict that last statement, there's no way to sell it here. If I have found a single truth in eastern Congo, it's that everyone has his or her own personal, localized version of it, and in this final account the FDLR are in shouting range of the righteous.

When we leave the shop half an hour later there is nothing to do but wait along the side of the road for the captain to call, but that quickly becomes uncomfortable. We all notice that people are staring, and that word from here to the bush travels fast. Whether it's me personally, or the car and the promise of money that comes with both, we make an easy target for the FDLR, or even for the soldiers. It's the great democratic force in eastern Congo, the one thing that everyone shares, regardless of ethnicity. Hutu or Tutsi, soldier or rebel, at some point everyone here knows what it means to feel vulnerable.

Walikale remains calm throughout the anniversary celebrations, just as Chuma and the UN had predicted. That evening, when an attack would be most likely, the village's main bar is packed with people and soldiers dancing together under a dim red light, with large bottles of Primus beer being passed around. The next day is a holiday as well, and even in the mining towns outside Bisie, all but a handful of the mineral comptoirs are closed. Tonnes of cassiterite and coltan (the essential minerals used in the manufacture of mobile phones and video games around the world) pass through here on normal days, yet with the exception of the tax post at the exit to the mine, there are no signs of wealth or profit and the town remains as poor as its neighbours. For years now, Congo's vast mineral resources have been exploited by the FDLR, by invading foreign countries including Rwanda and Uganda, and by corrupt elements within the Congolese military perpetuating the country's instability and keeping the eastern region awash in small arms. A plane touches down at midday on the tarmac road between the two principal mining towns; a small bribe to the guards buys us access to the road to watch from a distance. The sight of a plane on the one tarmac road in the region is so incongruous with the surrounding reality that it appears to be an almost covert operation. It is in fact utterly mundane; this plane is one of roughly a dozen that touches down on an average day to exchange bottles of beer and soda for white sacks of minerals that will be flown off to Bukavu or Goma before being released into the world – proof that there are massive profits being made from, instead of in, eastern Congo. A few weeks later, FDLR and indigenous rebel forces will attack the same airstrip, making off with an Indian co-pilot and the plane's entire cargo, again proof, if further were needed, that the rebels need not profit from the mines directly; there are countless other ways to get what they want. Two weeks later, the FDLR, along with their local counterparts, arrive by the hundreds to occupy an entire village for at least three days. They will take everything they want, and then return later to rape an estimated 500 women, along with some men and boys, day and night, often in groups, in front of children, because the government soldiers who were once there have left and because, for reasons that will most likely never be adequately explained, the UN forces, only a couple of dozen kilometres away, will never intervene.

The brutality of the attack in Walikale has one measurable effect: it finally leads to the arrest of Callixte Mbarushimana, the last of the FDLR commanders living safely in Europe. Mbarushimana is arrested in Paris, recalling Murwanashyaka's arrest eight months earlier in Germany. It is almost certainly not the last of the FDLR. There are still soldiers in Congo and supporters abroad. Its leaders in exile were not so much the source of the FDLR's strength, but symbolic of it. Exile, like any vacuum, needs to be filled, and the FDLR have done just that. ■

CONTACTS

Adam Broomberg & Oliver Chanarin

The Belfast Exposed Archive occupies a small room on the first floor at 23 Donegal Street and contains over 14,000 black-and-white contact sheets, documenting the Troubles from the early 1970s. These are photographs taken by professional photojournalists and 'civilian' photographers that chronicle protests, funerals and acts of terrorism as well as the more ordinary stuff of life: drinking tea; kissing girls; watching trains. Belfast Exposed was founded in 1983 as an antidote to concern over the careful control of images depicting British military activity during the Troubles.

Each photograph, rather like an Eastern miniature painting, offers up a self-contained universe all of its own; a small moment of desire, frustration or thwarted communication that is reanimated here after many years in darkness. The marks on the surface of the contact strips – across the image itself – allude to the presence of many visitors. These include successive archivists, who have ordered, catalogued and re-catalogued this jumble of images.

For many years the archive was made available to members of the public and sometimes they would deface their own image with a marker pen, ink or scissors. So in addition to the marks made by generations of archivists, photo editors, legal aids and activists, the traces of these very personal obliterations are also visible. They are the gestures of those who wished to remain anonymous. ■

THE MERCIES

Ann Patchett

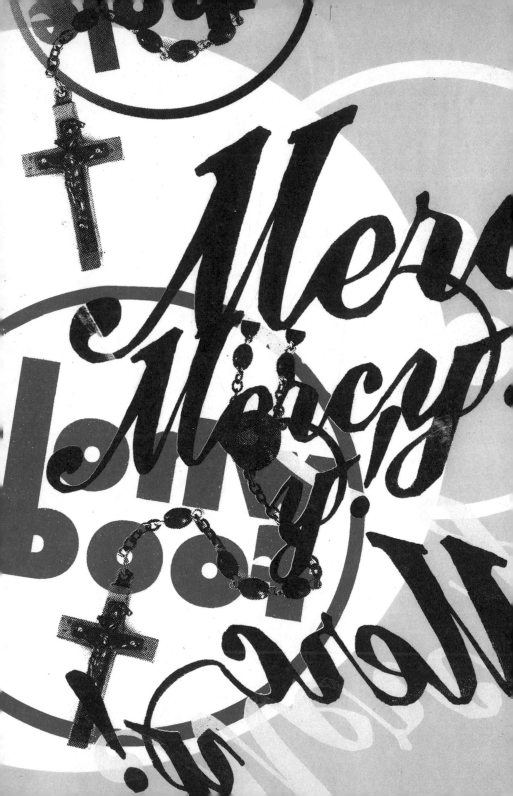

L ong before any decisions have been made about where or when she might be moving, Sister Nena starts combing the liquor stores early in the morning looking for boxes. She is breaking down the modest contents of her life into three categories: things to keep, things to throw away, things to donate to Catholic charities. Sister Melanie is doing the same.

'What's the rush?' I ask, picking my way past the long row of boxes that lines the front hall, everything labelled and sealed and neatly stacked. It is August, and the heat and humidity have turned the air into an unbearable soup. I think they're getting ahead of themselves and I tell them so. Sister Kathy, who is responsible for assessing their situation, won't be coming from the mother house in North Carolina for weeks.

'We've got to be ready,' Sister Nena says. She does not stop working. Her state of being is one of constant action, perpetual motion. A small gold tennis racket dangles from her neck where on another nun one would expect to find a cross. 'I won't pack the kitchen until the very end.'

Not that the kitchen matters. I suspect that the nuns, who are small enough to emulate the very sparrows God has His eye on, should be eating more, which is why I've brought them dinner. Sister Melanie is going to Mercy, the nuns' retirement home, but she doesn't know when. Some days she is looking forward to the move, other days she isn't so sure. She stops and looks in the bag at the casserole I've brought, gives me a hug, and ambles off again.

Sister Nena is certain that she doesn't want to go to Mercy. She regards it as the end of the line. She's hoping to land in a smaller apartment by herself, or maybe with another sister, though finding a new room-mate at the age of seventy-eight can be a challenge. 'It's up to God,' she says, then she goes back to her boxes.

Sister Nena was born in Nashville, the city where we both live. She was eighteen when she entered the convent. Sixty years later the convent is gone and the Sisters of Mercy who are left in this city are largely scattered. For almost twenty years, Sister Nena and Sister Melanie have lived in a condo they once shared with Sister Helen. The condo, which is within walking distance of the mall, is in an upscale suburban neighbourhood called Green Hills. It isn't exactly the place I would have pictured nuns living, but then everything about my friendship with Sister Nena has made me re-evaluate how life is for nuns these days.

'It's like that book,' she said, summing up the best-seller. 'First I pray, then I eat.'

'That leaves love,' I said.

'That's it. I love a lot of people. Pray, eat, love, tennis. I'm in a rut. I need to find something else I can do for others.'

I guess I always thought the rut was part of it. A religious life is not one that I associate with great adventure. But now that change is barrelling towards her, Sister Nena is restless for its arrival. Day after day she is standing up to meet it and I can see she's had a talent for adventure all along. It seems to me that entering the convent at the age of eighteen is in fact a great act of daring.

'I didn't always want to be a nun,' Sister Nena said. 'Not when I was younger. I wanted to be a tennis player. My brothers and I knew a man who let us play on his court in return for keeping it up. It was a dirt court and my brothers would roll it out with the big roller and I would repaint the lines. We played tennis every day.' Nena, the youngest of three. Nena, the only girl, following her brothers to the courts every morning of summer on her bicycle, racket in hand.

When I asked her what her brothers thought of her joining the convent, she said they thought she was crazy, using the word crazy as if it were a medical diagnosis. 'So did my father. He thought I was making a terrible mistake giving up getting married, having kids. I liked kids,' she said. 'I babysat a lot when I was young. I had a happy life back then. I had a boyfriend. His family was in the meat-packing business. My father called him Ham Boy. It was all good but still there was something that wasn't quite right. I didn't feel comfortable. I never felt like I was living the life I was supposed to.'

What about her mother is what I want to know. What did her mother say?

Sister Nena smiled the smile of a daughter who had pleased the mother she loved above all else. 'She was proud of me.'

There will never be enough days for me to ask Sister Nena all the things I want to know, and she is endlessly patient with me. She can see it plainly herself: it hasn't been an ordinary life. Some of my questions are surely a result of the leftover curiosity of childhood, the quiet suspicion that nuns were not like the rest of us. But there is another way in which the questions feel like an attempt to gather vital information for my own life. Forget about the yoga practice, the meditating, the vague dreams of going to an ashram in India: Sister Nena has stayed in Tennessee and devoted her life to God. She has lived with her calling for so long that it seems less a religious vocation than a marriage, a deeply worn path of mutual acceptance. Sister Nena and God understand one another. They are in it for life.

The Sisters of Mercy was started by Catherine McAuley in Dublin. She recognized the needs of poor women and girls and used her considerable inheritance to open a home for them called Mercy House, taking her vows in 1831. Committing your life to God was one thing, but I think that choosing an order would be akin to choosing which branch of the military to sign up for. Army? Navy? Dominicans? From a distance it all looks like service but the daily life must play out in very different ways. 'The Mercies taught me in school,' Sister Nena said.

I nod my head, of course. I was also taught by the Mercies in school. I was taught by Sister Nena.

'They never manipulated me,' she said in their defence. 'But I admired them, their goodness.'

I spent twelve years with the Sisters of Mercy and I am certain, in all that time, no one ever suggested that I or any of my friends should consider joining the order. Nuns have never been in the business of recruitment, which may in part account for their dwindling ranks. What we were told repeatedly was to *listen*. God had a vocation for all of us and if we paid close attention and were true to ourselves, we would know His intention. Sometimes you might not like what you heard. You might think that what was being asked of you was too much, but at that point there really was no getting out of it. Once you knew what God wanted from your life, you would have to be ten different kinds of fool to look the other way. When I was a girl in Catholic school I was open to the idea of being a nun, a mother, a wife, but whenever I closed my eyes and listened (and there was plenty of time for listening – in chapel, in math class, in basketball games – we were told the news could come at any time), the voice I heard was consistent: be a writer. It didn't matter that writing had never been listed as one of our options. I knew that for me this was the truth, and to this end I found the nuns to be invaluable examples. I was, after all, educated by a group of women who had in essence jumped ship, ignored the strongest warnings of their fathers and brothers in order to follow their own clear direction. They were working women who had given every aspect of their lives over to their beliefs, as I had every intention of giving my life over to my belief. The nun's existence was not so far from the kind of singular life I imagined for myself, even if God wasn't the object of my devotion.

In her years as a postulant and then a novice, Sister Nena moved around: Memphis, Cincinnati, Knoxville, finishing her education and taking her orders. When I asked her when she stopped wearing a habit, she had to think about it. '1970?' Her hair is now a thick, curling grey cut close to her head. 'I liked the habit. If they told us tomorrow we had to wear it again I'd be fine with that. Just not those things that went around the face. There was so much starch in them that they hurt.' She touched her cheek at the memory. 'It got so hot in the summer with all that stuff on, you couldn't believe it. But if it got too hot I'd just pull my skirts up.'

It was around 1969 that Sister Nena came back to Nashville to teach at St Bernard's Academy, about the same time I arrived from California and enrolled in first grade late that November. This is the point at which our lives first intersect: Sister Nena, age thirty-two, and Ann, very nearly six.

The convent where we met was an imposing and unadorned building of the darkest red brick imaginable. In those days it sat on the top of a hill and looked down over a long, rolling lawn dotted with statuary. It was there I learned to roller-skate and ran the three-legged race with Trudy Corbin on field day. Once a year I was part of a procession of little girls who set a garland of roses on top of the statue of Mary while singing, 'Oh Mary, we crown thee with blossoms today', then we would file back inside and eat our lunches out of paper sacks. The cafeteria was in the basement of the convent; the classrooms were on the first floor. On the second floor there was a spectacular chapel painted in bright blue. It had an altar made from Italian marble and a marble kneeling rail and rows of polished pews where I would go in the morning to say part of the rosary and then chat God up in that personal way that became popular after Vatican II. My mother worked long shifts as a nurse and she would take me and my sister to the convent early and pick us up late. The nuns would let us come into their kitchen and sort the silverware, which in retrospect I imagine they mixed together just to give us something to do. My sister and I were well aware of the privilege we were receiving, getting to go into their kitchen, their dining room, and, on very rare occasions, into the sitting room on the second floor where they had a television set. Still, in all those years, I never set foot on the third or fourth floor of the building. That was where the nuns slept, where Sister Nena slept, and it was for us as far away as the moon, even as it sat right on top of us.

How did we find each other again?' Sister Nena asked me recently while we were in the grocery store.

'You called me,' I said. 'Years ago. You were looking for money.'

She stopped in the middle of the aisle and shook her head. 'I forgot. It was for St Vincent's School. Oh, that's awful. It's awful that that's why I called you.'

I put my arm over her shoulder while she steered the cart. Sister Nena likes to steer the cart. 'At least you called.'

Sister Nena lived in the convent at St Bernard's until she was sixty years old. That was when the order sold the building. The parcel of land, which sat smack in the middle of a hip and crowded neighbourhood, was valuable. A large apartment complex was built in the front yard where we had played. They ripped out the giant mock orange trees first. Picking up mock oranges, which were smelly and green and had deep turning folds that were distressingly reminiscent of human brains, was a punishment all the girls sought to avoid. It surprised me how sorry I was to see the trees go.

The convent had an interior window over the doorway to the chapel that could be opened on to the third floor so that the nuns who were too infirm to come downstairs could sit in their wheelchairs and listen to Mass. When I was a girl I would try to glance up at them without being noticed. From my vantage point down in the pews they were tiny in their long white dresses, which may have been the uniform of advanced age and may have just been their nightgowns. After the sale of the convent, the sisters who were retired or needed care were sent to Mercy, which was then a new facility twenty miles outside of town. The grade-school students were moved next door into the building that had once been the high school (the high school, never as successful as the grade school, was now defunct) and the convent itself was converted into office spaces. Every schoolroom and nun's bedroom found another use: a therapist's office, a legal practice, a Pilates studio. The altar was given to a parish in Stone Mountain, Georgia. It had to be taken out through the back wall with a crane. The pews were sold. The empty chapel was now rented out for parties.

'That was hard,' Sister Nena said in the manner of one used to taking hard things in stride. 'We had a lot of fun there, especially in the summers when everyone would come home, the sisters who taught in other towns would all come back. We'd sit up and tell stories and laugh, have a glass of wine.'

I went back to St Bernard's once, years later, and climbed the back stairs to the fourth floor and stood in an empty bedroom/office to look out of the window. It was like looking down from the moon.

The vows for the Sisters of Mercy are poverty, celibacy and obedience, service to the poor, sick and uneducated, with perseverance until death. Obedience is another way of saying that you don't complain when your order decides to sell the place where you live. You don't get a vote. Sometimes this strikes me as ridiculously unfair ('You should have told them no,' I find myself wanting to say, even though I have no idea who 'them' might have been). Other times, when I can manage to see outside the limitations of my own life, I catch a glimpse of what the move must have been for Sister Nena: another act of faith, the belief that God has a plan and is looking after you. It must be the right thing because you had turned your life over to God and even if you didn't understand all the intricacies of the deal, He wasn't about to make a mistake.

After the sale, the younger sisters, the ones who were still teaching, were relocated to rented apartments around town so they could have an easier commute into work. 'It was all right,' Sister Nena said. 'We'd all still get together on the weekends and have dinner.' Sister Nena, who taught reading in grades one through three, and Sister Helen, my math teacher for those same grades, and Sister Melanie, the lower-school principal, lived together in a rented condo, the three bedrooms making a straight line off the upstairs hallway. They were happy there. They continued to work until the time came to work less. They semi-retired, retired, tutored children who needed tutoring, helped out at Catholic charities. After she left St Bernard's, Sister

Nena volunteered at St Vincent de Paul's, a school for underserved African American children in north Nashville that remained in a state of constant financial peril until it finally went under.

Then, in 2004, Sister Helen had a stroke. After she got out of the hospital she was sent to Mercy. For a long time Sister Melanie and Sister Nena thought that she'd come home and take up her place again in the third bedroom, but Sister Helen only got worse. Day after day, Sister Nena would drive the twenty miles out to Mercy to visit her friend and try to get her to do the puzzles in the children's math workbooks that she had taught from for years, and sometimes Sister Helen would, but mostly she would sit and watch television. Over time she recognized Sister Nena less and less, and then finally not at all. It was because of the stroke that I started seeing more of Sister Nena. We would have lunch after she played tennis or have coffee in the afternoons. She would talk about her friend and sometimes she would cry a little. They had, after all, been together for a very long time. It was during one of those conversations that she mentioned Sister Helen's last name was Kain, and I wondered how I could have never known that before.

Sister Nena and Sister Melanie stayed on in Green Hills, but by 2010 Sister Melanie was growing increasingly fragile, forgetful. It was the consensus among the other nuns, and of Sister Melanie herself, that she was ready to go out to Mercy.

The question then was what should be done with Sister Nena? She was, after all, still playing tennis like one of the Williams sisters three times a week and didn't seem like a candidate for the retirement home. Still, while one spare bedroom could be overlooked, the rented condo was $1,400 a month and there were no extra nuns to fill up what would now be two spare bedrooms. It was decided that Sister Nena could stay out of Mercy, but she needed to find an apartment that was significantly less expensive. For the first time in her life she would be on her own.

I like to take Sister Nena to Whole Foods. It is a veritable amusement park of decadence and wonder to one who has taken a vow of poverty. Her ability to cook is rudimentary at best and she doesn't like to shop, so I advocate prepared foods from the deli. Sister Melanie, who adored the grocery store, made her pilgrimage to Kroger every Sunday. It was not a habit Sister Nena planned on picking up, claiming her Italian heritage would save her: as long as she had a box of pasta and a jar of sauce she was never going to starve. I could usually convince her to let me get a few things now that I knew what she liked. She was greatly enamoured of the olive bar. After Sister Kathy had visited and the decision about everyone's future was settled, I took Sister Nena to the store and we got some coffee and went to sit at a small table by the window to discuss the details. She told me she'd found a place in a sprawling complex called Western Hills on the other side of town. I didn't like the sound of it. I knew the neighbourhood, and the busy street was crowded with fast-food places, cheque-cashing centres and advertisements for bail bondsmen. She was set on getting a two-bedroom so that she could have a little office for her computer and the chair where she says her prayers in the morning. I argued for a smaller place in the neighbourhood where she lived now, but for once in her life the decision was Sister Nena's to make and she intended to get what she wanted. 'It's all going to be fine,' she said, trying to reassure me, to reassure herself. 'Sister Jeannine lives out there. She likes the place. I've got it all figured out. Sister Melanie's helping me work on a budget. They gave me a bank account, a credit card and a debit card.'

There in the cafe at Whole Foods, amid the swirl of mothers with strollers and young men with backpacks, my friend was not out of place, a slightly built Italian woman in a tracksuit. I stared at her blankly, unsure of what we were talking about.

'I got a checking account,' she said again.

'You've never had a checking account?'

She shook her head. 'Melanie handled all the finances. She paid the bills.' Then Sister Nena leaned in, moving her cup aside. 'What exactly is the difference between a credit card and a debit card?'

I tried to outline the differences as clearly as possible; explaining the different ways either one of them can trip a person up. 'When you use the debit card you have to write it down in the registry the same way you would a cheque. You need to write everything down and then subtract it from your balance each time so you'll know how much you have.'

She took a sip of her coffee. 'I can do that. I'm smart enough.'

'You're perfectly smart,' I said. 'But I don't know if you know all of this already. Once a month you get a statement from the bank. You have to balance your chequebook against the bank statement.' I never thought much of the intellectual content of my secondary education, which was weighed down by a preponderance of religion classes and gym. But while the nuns may have been short on Shakespeare, they were long on practicality. By the time we were in high school we had learned how to make stews and sauces and cakes. We knew how to make crêpes. We could remove stains and operate a washing machine. We were taught not only the fundamentals of sewing, but how to make a budget and balance a chequebook, how to fill out a simple tax form. Down at the grade school, Sister Nena had not received the benefits of any of these lessons.

She puzzled over what I was saying about bank statements for a long time. When I got to the part about how she was supposed to mark off her cancelled cheques in the tiny column in the registry, she suddenly perked up as if she had found the answer to the problem. Then she started laughing. 'You shouldn't tease me like that,' she said, putting her hand on her heart. 'You scared me to death. You shouldn't tease a nun.'

'I'm not teasing you,' I said.

By the slight flash of panic that came across her face I could tell that she believed me. Still, she shook her head. 'I don't have to do that. I never saw Sister Melanie do that.'

All the Sisters of Mercy living in their separate apartments submit a budget to the mother house, estimating the cost of their electric and phone bills, food and rent. What they came up with for their monthly stipend was a modest number at best. The order picks that up, along with all medical expenses and insurance. When Sister Nena was hit two years ago by a car that ran a red light, her car was totalled and the order agreed that she could have a new car. I drove her to the Toyota dealership. All she had to do was sign a piece of paper and pick up the keys. 'I hope it's not red,' she said on the way there. 'I don't like red cars.'

The car, a Corolla, was new, and it was red. Sister Nena walked a slow circle around it, studying, while the salesman watched. It wasn't every day a car was purchased over the phone for someone who hadn't seen it. 'I take it back,' she said to me finally. 'The red is nice.'

When Sister Nena was a young nun teaching at St Bernard's, around the time that I was her student, she received an allowance from the order of twenty dollars a month. All of her personal expenses were to be covered by that sum: Life Savers, shoes, clothing. Any cash gifts from the parents of students that came inside Christmas cards were to be turned over, as was any money from her own parents folded into birthday cards. It wasn't a matter of the order leeching up the presents; it was the enactment of the vow. They were still to be poor even when a little extra cash presented itself. I couldn't help but wonder if there was ever a small temptation to take a ten-dollar bill from one's own birthday card, but the question seemed impolite. 'What if your mother sent you a sweater?' I asked instead. I was not being wilfully obtuse. I was trying to figure out the system.

'Oh, that wasn't a problem. You got to keep the sweater.'

It is possible that the only reason any of this makes some limited sense to me is because these were the lessons I was taught as a child. The notion of a rich man's camel not being able to make its way through the eye of the needle was a thought so terrifying (my family was not without means) it would keep me up at night. I believed then that turning away from the material world was the essence of freedom, and someplace deep inside myself; someplace that very rarely sees the light of day. I still believe it now. I imagine that no one who has spent sixty years embracing the tenets of poverty thinks to herself, I wish I'd had a $200 bottle of perfume. That said, after our coffee and the perilous conversation about checking accounts, we went into Whole Foods to do some shopping. Sister Nena was adamant about wanting to go to Kroger, a less expensive grocery store a few blocks away, because the weekly nun dinner was going to be at her house that night and she'd promised to make pork chops. I told her no, I was buying the pork chops where we were. I believed that pork chops were not an item that should be bargain-hunted.

'When did you get to be so bossy?' she said to me.

'I've been waiting my entire life to boss you around,' I said. I filled up the cart with salads and bread and good German beer while Sister Nena despaired over how much money I spent.

In the checkout line I was still thinking about the twenty dollars a month, a figure that she told me was later raised to one hundred. 'I worked almost fifty years and I never once saw a pay cheque,' she said, and then she shrugged as if to say she hadn't really missed it.

Sister Melanie had moved out to Mercy the week before Sister Nena moved to her new apartment, but she came back to help. Sister Nena's eighty-year-old brother, Bud, was there along with two of his children, Andy and Pam, and Sister Nena's friend Nora came. Together we loaded up our cars with everything Sister Nena didn't want to leave to the two movers. It was six thirty in the morning and had just started to rain.

'We can probably take all the boxes in the cars,' she said. 'That way the movers wouldn't have to bother with them.'

'They're movers,' I said, trying to remember if I had helped a friend move since I was in graduate school. 'That's what they do.' I went to take apart Sister Nena's computer, which was a series of enormous black metal boxes with dozens of snaking cables coming out the back. It looked like something that might have come out of NASA in the seventies. I was very careful putting it in my car.

Western Hills was actually set farther back from the busy street than I had realized, and the complex was so big that it had the insulated feel of a small, walled city. Once our caravan arrived and the contents of our cars were emptied out into the apartment's small living room, the rest of the group went back to their lives and Sister Nena, Sister Melanie, Sister Jeannine and I begin to put the food in the refrigerator and the clothes in closets while the movers brought in the furniture and the boxes. The three nuns, all in their seventies, did hard work at a steady pace, and while I might have been tempted to sit down for a moment on the recently positioned sofa, they did not, and so I did not. I told the movers where to put the television.

'I'm sorry,' the young man said to me. 'I know you told me your name but I don't remember.'

'Ann,' I said.

'Sister Ann?' he asked.

It was true that in a room with three nuns I could easily pass for the fourth. We were all dressed in jeans and sweatshirts. We had all forgone mascara. I shook my head. 'Just Ann,' I said. I thought about my mother, who, like the nuns, is in her seventies now. She was and is a woman of legendary beauty, a woman with a drawer full of silk camisoles and a closet full of high-heeled shoes, who never left the house without make-up even if she was just walking the dog. My sister and I often wondered how her particular elegance and attention to detail had passed over us, how we had managed so little dexterity where beauty was concerned. But as I talked to the mover, a Catholic kid with a shamrock tattooed inside his wrist, I thought of how we would arrive at the convent very early in the morning and how we would stay sometimes until after dark. Maybe what rubbed off over the years was more than faith. Maybe the reason I felt so comfortable with Sister Nena and the rest of the nuns was that I spent the majority of the waking hours of my childhood with them.

That first time Sister Nena called me all those years ago, when she was looking for someone to help her buy school supplies for the children at the St Vincent de Paul School, she told me she had prayed about it for a long time before picking up the phone. She wasn't happy about having to ask for money, but the children didn't have paper or crayons or glue sticks and she knew I'd been doing well over the years. She'd read some of my books. 'I taught you how to read and write,' she said.

'You did,' I said, and didn't mention that she had in fact done a great deal more for me than that. Sister Nena had been the focal point of all of my feelings of persecution, the repository for my childish anger. I knew that she had thought I was lazy and slow, dull as a butter knife. I watched the hands of other girls shoot up in class while I sat in the back, struggling to understand the question. While having no evidence to the contrary at the time, I was certain that I was smarter than she gave me credit for being, and I would prove it. I grew up wanting to be a writer so that Sister Nena would realize she had underestimated me. I have always believed that the desire for revenge is one of life's great motivators, and my revenge against Sister Nena would be my success. When I was a child I dreamed that one day she would need something from me and I would give it to her with full benevolence. It was true that she had taught me how to read and write, but what she didn't mention on the phone that day, and what she surely didn't remember after nearly fifty years of teaching children, was what an excruciatingly long time it had taken me to learn.

My parents divorced in Los Angeles where I had started first grade at the Cathedral of the Incarnation. In late November of that year, my mother took my sister and me to Tennessee for what was going to be a three-week vacation to see a man she knew there. We never went back. I had not yet learned to read in California and when I was eventually enrolled in St Bernard's, I landed on Sister Nena's doorstep. I remember her well. She was child-sized herself, wearing a plain blue polyester dress that zipped up the back. She had short dark hair and the perpetual tan of a person who played tennis on any passable day. She moved through the classroom with enormous energy and purpose and I could all but see the nonsensical letters of the alphabet trailing behind her wherever she went. I was perilously lost for all the long hours of the school day, but I had yet to conclude that I was in any real trouble. It was still a time in my life when I believed we would go home again and I would catch up among the children and the nuns I knew in California. In Nashville, we stayed in the guest room of strangers, friends of my mother's friend. These people, the Harrises, had daughters of their own who went to St Bernard's and the daughters were not greatly inclined to go to school, nor were the Harrises inclined to make them. Many days we all stayed home together. It was 1969, a fine year for truancy.

I started second grade at St Bernard's as well, having learned very few of the lessons that had been laid out in my first year. The enrolment at the school was small and we had the same teachers for grades one through three. Again, Sister Helen was there with the math I didn't understand. Again, Sister Nena rolled up her sleeves, but the making of letters eluded me. We left the Harrises' house and found our own apartment, and then moved again. After Christmas we moved to Mufreesboro, a less expensive town thirty minutes away where I was enrolled in public school, but we didn't stay. A few months into third grade we were back in Nashville and I was back with Sister Nena. I still couldn't read whole sentences or write the alphabet with all the letters facing in the right direction. I knew a handful of words and I did my best to fake my way through. Sister Nena, seeing me turn up for a half-year of school for the third time in a row, had had enough. She kept me in from recess and after school, badgering me with flashcards and wide-ruled paper on which I was expected to write out letters neatly over and over again. If I was firmly wedged between the cracks I'd fallen into, she had plans to pull me up, by the hair if necessary. She would see to it that I wasn't going to spend the rest of my life not exactly knowing how to read or write. Cursive was waiting just ahead in fourth grade, she told me. I had better get up to speed. She might as well have said that in fourth grade classes would be conducted in French (a confusion that came from a Babar book my sister had. Because it was both in cursive and in French I believed that cursive *was* French). I was terrified of all there was to do, of how far behind I had fallen, and somehow I convinced myself that I was terrified of Sister Nena. I wouldn't be in trouble if it wasn't for her because no one else in my life had noticed I couldn't read.

The only thing interesting about my anger and blame of Sister Nena was my willingness to hold on to it without any further reflection until I was in my thirties. I had let my seven-year-old self, my eight-year-old self, make my case against her. How much happier I would have been never to learn anything at all! It wasn't until I sent her a cheque for school supplies that I found myself wondering how often I was in her classroom those first three years and how much work she had in front of her every time I wandered in. It isn't often the past picks up the telephone and calls, affording the opportunity to reconsider personal history in a way that could save countless thousands of dollars in therapy had I been inclined to go. I found myself thinking about my childhood, my education. It is a pastime I am particularly loath to engage in, but I was struck that all I had remembered was her exasperation with my epic slowness, not her ultimate triumph over it. To overstate the case, it was a bit akin to Helen Keller holding a grudge against Annie Sullivan for yanking her around. The next time the children of St Vincent de Paul ran out of glue sticks and Sister Nena called me again, I suggested that we go shopping together and buy some.

She was standing outside her condo in Green Hills when I arrived, waiting for me. Sister Melanie and Sister Helen, still in good health, were home as well. Tennis and prayer and a habit of eating very little must agree with the human body because Sister Nena seemed to have forgone the ageing process completely. She was exactly the person I had known when I was a child and she was nothing like that person at all. She opened up her arms and held me. I was one of her students, one of who knows how many children that had passed through her classroom. That was what she remembered about me. I was one of her own.

There have been very few things in my life that have made me as happy as taking Sister Nena shopping. When we started it was all school supplies, though eventually she confessed her longing to buy small presents for the teachers at St Vincent's who were every bit as poor as their students and paid a sliver of the wages a public-school teacher would have made. She picked out bottles of hand lotion and boxes of Kleenex, staplers and Life Savers, gifts too modest to embarrass anyone, but her joy over having something to give them all but vibrated as we walked up and down the aisles of Target piling things into our cart. It turned out the real heartbreak of the vow of poverty was never being able to buy presents for the people who were so clearly in need.

Despite my constant questions about what she might need for herself, it was years before Sister Nena let me buy anything for her. She wouldn't dream of letting me take her to the olive bar back then. That came later in our friendship, after Sister Helen had her stroke, after her best friend Joanne died of cancer, which was an inconceivable loss. We inched towards each other slowly over many years. At some point I realized that the people she was closest to were dying off or being sent away. Over the course of years there was a place for me.

'You're at the top of my prayer list,' she tells me. 'And not because you buy me things.' She has come to understand that letting me buy her things makes me ridiculously happy, and my happiness, instead of the things themselves, is the source of her joy.

'I know,' I said.

'It's because I love you,' she said.

So ferocious is my love for Sister Nena that I can scarcely understand it myself. Hers is the brand of Catholicism I remember from my childhood, a religion of good work and very little discussion.

'I like the Catholic Church,' she says to me sometimes.

'Good thing,' I say, which always makes her laugh. I think that she is everything I had ever loved about our religion distilled down to fit into one person, the part of the faith that is both selfless and responsible: bringing soup to the sick, going to visit the widower husbands of her friends who have died, sticking with the children who are slow to learn and teaching them how to read, because it wasn't just me, it turns out there are legions of us. She babysits for two Haitian girls, Islande and Thania, and helps them with their reading and their math. They ask their mother to bring the phone to their beds before they go to sleep so they can call Sister Nena and say goodnight, tell her they have said their prayers. I think of how Sister Nena spoke of the Mercies who taught her in school and how she had admired their goodness. I think of how it took me half my life to comprehend the thing she had discovered as a child (I have no doubt that she had been a better student than I was).

She is happy in her new apartment, though she probably could have set up her camp in a closet somewhere and been fine. Happiness is her mindset, her decision, and while she often reminds me that God will take care of things, she is also determined not to trouble Him if at all possible. It's a little bit like wanting to move all the boxes before the movers come. She will take on the work of her life quickly, do it all herself when no one is watching so that she can show God how little help she needs.

Any worries she has these days are focused on Sister Melanie, who is adjusting slowly to her new life at Mercy. Sister Melanie is shy and had long relied on Sister Nena for her social skills. 'She stays in her room all the time,' Sister Nena said. 'Whenever I go out to see her, there she is. I tell her, no one's going to find you in here. You have to get out.' She is reaching down into that place where Sister Melanie has wedged herself. She is trying to pull her up.

We got together the day after the funeral of her friend Mary Ann. Mary Ann was the other Catholic in her tennis group. 'I'm fine. I'm not sad,' Sister Nena tells me when I call. I know better than to believe her. 'You don't have to take me out.'

'What if I just want to see you?' I say.

Over lunch she tells me that the last time she saw her, Mary Ann was very peaceful. 'She looked at me and said, "Nena, I'm ready. I want to see God."' Then Sister Nena shook her head. 'I'm wrong. That was the time before last. The last time I saw her she couldn't say anything. When I went to her funeral and I saw the urn there, I thought, where is her soul?' Sister Nena looks at me then, hoping that I might know. 'Is it with God? I want to believe her soul is with God. She was so certain. I'm just not sure. I shouldn't say that.' She puts her hand flat out on the table. 'I am sure.'

'Nobody's sure,' I say.

'Sister Jeannine is sure.' She shakes her head. 'I don't know. I'm contradicting myself. I know God made us but I'm not so sure about what happens afterwards.'

'What do you want to happen?' I ask her.

This she knows the answer to immediately. It is as if she has been waiting her entire lifetime for someone to ask her. 'I want God to hold me,' she says.

You above all others, I tell her. You first. ∎

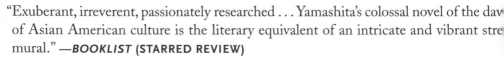

JAMES

Madeleine Thien

Sorya tries to make the bed with him still in it. This, he knows, is her quiet way of telling him that it's past noon and a man should not be so slovenly. He doesn't like speaking Khmer in the morning, before breakfast, so he addresses her in English. *Let me sleep a little longer.* She brings him a cup of coffee and he feels like a wet-nosed boy home sick from school. Her fingertips smell of anise. He drinks, burns his tongue, and then he pulls her back into bed with him, strips her, fucks her, tells her to forget everything but him. He says this in English and she answers in Khmer. In the end they speak the same loopholed language that says only a little and lets the big things slide through.

'James,' she had said when they first met. 'What a serious name.'

She is clever and fearless, she married him for practical reasons, and she will never be completely grateful. Sorya doesn't stay in bed past 6 a.m. What she does, he can't imagine. The schools are closed and have been for months, so she has no job to report to.

He remembers the days they went to the discotheque; Dararith bought the beer but they gambled with James's cash. Dararith steered the moped that ferried them around but usually James and Sorya had to walk home without him, picking their way through the rubble. He pursued women as if they were keys on a ring, and he was always falling in love because his brand of affection was endearingly sudden. Sorya was glamorous with her black hair loose and her bare shoulders and calf-high boots, her market-stall clothing that she wore like high fashion. Television, she told him, on one of those awkward walks home, can be a gifted teacher. And books. She married James, maybe, for his books. Something to distract her while she waited for her brother to come back, but it's been two years and it's obvious by now that people don't come back.

She doesn't wear make-up any more but her hair is still long. Unbrushed, it floods around her and it seems, to James, as if it eats the light and hides the things that no one says: I married you as a favour to Dararith; I married you because of the war, out of loneliness, out of fear. I love only you. They both think these things; they both hold themselves in reserve.

'James,' she says now. 'It's a good name but it doesn't suit you.'

'King James.'

She pushes the covers aside, stands up. When did she get so thin, so melancholy?

'Don't leave me,' he tells her but then he is suddenly embarrassed. 'I hate sleeping alone,' he explains and she turns, a half-smile on her face, a half-sadness.

The war was ending and he worked all the time. The storehouses were empty; he had no medicine, no needles, saline or chloroquine, no bandages, no aspirin or dysentery pills. He patted shoulders, amputated limbs, blinked into the persistent heat, and turned his back on the worst cases. It was the cool season, supposedly, but his clothes were sweat-drenched by ten in the morning. In his gut was a feeling of panic mixed with the weight of inertia, he was light-headed and joyous and bitterly angry. The radio spewed bulletins from the war in Vietnam and the shaming of the Americans not only there but here in Cambodia and next door in Laos. Ask the diplomats – American, French, English – and this humiliation was everyone's fault but their own. Ask the Cambodians what would happen next and they just shrugged and smiled their fatalistic smiles. James hoped it was the last time he would live in a place where no one carried any responsibility, where the days were predetermined by the hundred lives already lived, by a thousand acts of karma, by destiny that rubbed out other destinations. He was sick of this country and he would have left already if it weren't for Sorya. That's what he tells himself. But every day he goes back to the camps and the Red Cross shelters and feels strangely at peace. Ten years ago he was smoking pot in a dive on Powell Street, coming home blinkered, but his mother and Hiroji, true innocents, never noticed a thing. When he gets high it reminds him of how the air burned his throat in Tokyo when he was small, how he was terrified of fire, and then the long journey by boat and plane and bus that took them to Vancouver where everything was green, where things were young and not skeletal, but still he was afraid.

His father had been a Professor of Medicine at Tokyo University, he had been a solemn, determined man, but the supreme effort of getting them out of defeated Japan had ruined his health. When his contacts in America disappointed him, he had turned to England. In the end, he settled for Canada. A year after they reached Vancouver, his father died, post-stroke, on a crisp, white bed in a Canadian hospital. James remembered the place well, the sharp, stingy smell of it and the squawk of rubber soles on the icy floors. Be brave, his father had told him, and all the while his kid brother had pressed his pink face against his mother's skin and slept in ignorant bliss.

His mother had opened a dry-goods shop on Powell Street and James had taken his first paper route, his first of many: the *Vancouver Sun*, the *Province*, the *Sing Tao Daily*. Hiroji used to lie on the mat in the back of the store and coo at them, and the baby's cooing made James feel improbably wise. He was eleven years old when he told his baby brother that they would both be doctors, real professionals. Maybe Tokyo and his father had given him a taste for calamity; maybe he had inherited his father's uneasy, chafing mind. He scraped through medical school, finished his residency. The Vietnam War was in full swing and he signed up with the Red Cross. When all hell broke loose, he preferred to be busy and not just standing around. Saigon was fine, but Cambodia is something else, manic-depressive, split with contradictions. They take him for a local here, a regular Chinese-Khmer slogging through the mud.

On the night he travelled from Phnom Penh to Neak Luong, he packed and unpacked three times, removing his camera, adding his journal. Removing bandages and adding chocolate and whiskey. Overhead, helicopters circled and he told Sorya, 'Maybe it's better if you come with me.'

'I don't think so,' she said.

He was on his way east and he realized she was right. Any day now, Neak Luong would fall to the Khmer Rouge. Probably he'd be shot by a sniper, or his boat would be shelled, or some hideous Communist maquis would poach him and serve him for supper.

'Write me a letter,' she said and they smiled because the postal system was a joke.

'Take this money,' James said, 'and buy us two tickets for Bangkok.'

'Honestly, you want to leave Phnom Penh? This heaven?'

'Do you?'

She laughed. 'All this time, I only stayed because of you.'

'Don't joke,' he said, confused.

'Careful in the wild,' she said. 'Don't come home dressed in black, carrying an AK and wearing rubber sandals. I'll shoot you on sight.'

'I'll come in a stampede of elephants.'

Her eyes teased him with restrained laughter. The foolish things he would do, the foolish dances he would perform, to make her laugh.

'In better days,' he said, 'we'll go to the sea.'

'Promise me.'

He saw the lines at the corners of her eyes, he heard something in her voice, a foreboding, a hopelessness he'd tried so hard to banish with bravado, with laughter. What other avenue was left them? Every day they were surrounded by corpses, women without faces, men without limbs.

'Yes,' he said. 'I do promise.'

They were ambushed in the dark. The cruddy boat tipped right then left, and James had a crushing sense of déjà vu as black-clothed creatures lifted from the water and slithered into the boat. He wondered whether Sorya would open the cache of money he had left her, whether any tickets remained for Bangkok, whether she would stay or go. For a split second, before the first kick, he thought he was being sent to join Dararith in the afterlife to which all doctors disappeared: a haven of arrogant, self-pitying men, a fate worse than hell. But this wasn't a joke. These creatures had no sense of irony. They beat him and he, a soft Canadian, was already begging for mercy after the first punch. They threw him into a hold. He thought of his father, who'd had the good sense to pass away in a clean bed rather than down in the reeking underground, in the terrifying Tokyo shelters, and now he, King James, would pass away in the dark, sucked into the careless water. One day he would wash up, bloated and unrecognizable, on to the shore of a shitty country. He heard them shoot the boat driver. He cried harder as they threw the body away.

They kept him blindfolded all the time. Once, when they took the blindfold off, they asked him to identify tablets they had found in his bags. The samples were pink, like cotton candy at the Pacific National Exhibition fairgrounds, like *champa* flowers, a pink that seemed foolish and innocent in this burned, exhausted landscape.

'These are vitamins,' he said. He answered them in Khmer and they said he was a spy and he said, 'No, I am not.'

'Where are you from?'

'Japan. Tokyo.'

'Where is your passport?'

'Lost.'

'Why are you here?'

'To treat the wounded.'

'The wounded?' they said, taunting him. 'You mean the Lon Nols, the traitors?'

He shook his head vehemently. 'I treat the people hurt by American bombs.'

They covered his eyes and returned him to darkness.

With the blindfold on, he felt absurdly safe. They surrounded him: bare feet on the thirsty ground, rifles smartly reloaded, the smell of a campfire. He heard someone getting a haircut, the scissors stuttering like a solitary cricket. He heard a fire starting and water boiling, he ate mushy gruel with his hands, he itched all over from the ants in the dirt, his tongue felt cracked. Night and day, his feet were shackled, he had to piss into a foul bamboo container, he was constipated. Everything hurt. He couldn't believe it was possible to be scared so long.

Sometimes, in his fantasies, he sits at his father's bedside. The blinds let in whiskers of light and he can see his father's right hand curled on the sheet, the skin over the knuckles flaccid and pale. He finds the doctors loud and the nurses kind and nobody really looks at him, not even his parents. James tells himself it's not possible to disappoint the dead. All that matters to the living is the living, that's what he had tried to explain to Sorya after her brother disappeared: 'If you have the chance to escape you have to take it. If I go missing, don't sit around like a fool.' He had felt like a hero when he said this.

But why waste words? Grieving Dararith, she had barely seemed to notice him. She just sat in the apartment thinking and reading, cleaning, cooking, disappearing. She didn't need his devotion and this independence, her strength made him feel confused and shiftless; it made him feel temporary, like an insect clinging to a drain.

Suddenly there were no more planes in the sky and no more shelling. They stopped moving around so frequently. The blindfold was removed and he found himself in a small, square storeroom, or it would have been a storeroom had there been anything on the shelves. It was comfortable enough. The floor had French cement tiles, dirty now, but the design had been lovely once. A short, efficient man came in to give him water, rice soup and, unexpectedly, a piece of soap. Eventually, the man started to extend his visits. He sat down on the floor and asked James questions about Phnom Penh, the Red Cross, about the war in Vietnam, about food and music and religion, about his wife, about Dararith. They always spoke in Khmer. James would sit with his arms tied behind his back while the man probed him, as if his life story were a confession, as if the two were the same thing.

The man was reedy, dark-skinned, with a way of tapping his knee rhythmically with his fingertips when he spoke. He studied the ground with such intensity that James found himself looking, too, at the tiled floor, taking in the stranger's soft hands, and then the Kalashnikov laid confidently between them, the barrel of the gun covered by the cadre's Chinese cap, as if in a decorative flourish.

One morning, the man surprised James. He said, 'Let me tell you about someone I once knew. A friend. I was studying at the Lycée Sisowath in Phnom Penh. Do you know it?'

'Everyone knows it.'

The man went on. 'This was more than twenty years ago. I lived with another boy, a Chinese-Khmer from Svay Rieng Province. Are you familiar with that area?'

'Of course.'

'You've been there?'

James nodded.

The man was impressed. 'His mother had a petrol stand,' he said, continuing. 'The father was dead. The boy, Kwan, drove a lorry and he would give me lifts around the city. He was raising money for his tuition and he worked all the time.'

The man's face was passive and kind, and it reminded James, disconcertingly, of his mother. His mother, too, had many surfaces, but he'd learned to see between the blinds, behind the clean edges.

'Kwan was trustworthy,' the man said. His voice dropped, not quite a whisper. 'Can I tell you that I trusted him more than the friends I went to school with? Those were lazy boys who never worked. Inside their empty heads they didn't even understand the concept of work. I started to tutor him. He got up very early to drive the lorry but in the afternoons, when everyone slept, I gave him lessons. He was quick. The thing about Kwan was, he was mute. He could read lips, he could adapt, but he never, ever spoke. I confess, I was fascinated by him. Boys my age were malleable. We swallowed each and every lesson without chewing it first. But Kwan, he was apart. He kept his thoughts to himself and he kept his peace.

'When you first arrived, I was astonished. I said to myself, Maybe Kwan got an education after all! Maybe he paid his way to medical school and made himself a gentleman. I congratulated myself that I, alone, had recognized you.'

A mosquito buzzed at James's cheek and he wondered how the insect had found its way into the locked room where there were no windows and the air was stale. It must have come in with the man.

'Are you Kwan?'

'No.'

Generously, the man extended his hand and hushed the mosquito away. 'Can you be certain?'

James didn't know what to say. Now there were insects thrumming nearby; in the ceiling corners they made a sound like a headache. Loose greenery was growing through hairline cracks in the wall, the colour too vivid for this room.

The man nodded, satisfied. 'Keep your peace, that's what I wanted to tell you. Just keep your peace for now.'

He gave James a new set of clothes, trousers and a loose shirt, faded black.

'What is this place?' James asked.

'Once it was a school,' the man said.

James waited for him to continue. The man just looked at him, tranquil, silent.

That night, the rains started. The grass in the wall dripped tiny beads of water. James felt unbearably cold. He remembered, one weekend, taking his brother to the Pacific Ocean. They had caught the ferry across the Strait of Georgia, and then driven the old Datsun to the western edge of Vancouver Island, through the shamelessly fat trees with their towering canopies. His brother, ten years younger, always wanted to hear about Tokyo, but James had little to say. He remembered the bomb shelters and the charred dog he saw once, and the brief sojourns home his father made, and how the war in China had sculpted his father into someone both powerful

and empty. His brother waited patiently and James just shrugged and said, *Fuck Japan.* The bottom of the Datsun was rusted through and the floor on the front-passenger side had a magnificent hole, you could see the asphalt blurring by: drop something and it was gone forever. How many things had they lost to that gaping hole? His house keys, Hiroji's plastic watch, apples tumbling from their grocery bags, all sorts of rubbish.

'But one day you'll take me to Tokyo, right, and show me things?'

'Show you what?' James had said, shrugging. 'I'll introduce you to the girls I knew when I was four.'

He could smell the sea through that hole long before they got there, the salt heaviness, the fresh green-ness of it. He loved the ocean no matter how desperately cold it was. He'd bought a wetsuit, a used one (he'd had no money for a new one), because he was addicted to the fury of the tide. Those currents knocked him back, they overpowered him, and yet he felt alive, not fragmented, not broken. He tried to explain this to Hiroji when they lay, that first night, in their one-season tent.

'It's religious,' he had said finally, lacking words.

Hiroji said, 'I like it too.'

In the narrow glow of the flashlight, Hiroji's face was round and small.

James wanted to tell him, 'I'm not your father. You don't have to look at me like that. You can yell at me and tell me I'm a fake.'

Instead he said, 'You didn't pack your schoolbooks, did you?'

Hiroji looked at him nervously. 'Just a few.'

'I'm going to lock them in the car.'

'Ha ha,' his brother said.

'Ha ha,' James answered.

The rain started. It drummed the ocean, it slipped through the high canopy of trees and reached their tent, a tapping of needles.

'Ichiro,' his brother said tentatively, 'do we need to sleep in the car?'

'No, brother,' James said. 'It's fine. I chose a good place for us.'

James reached his fingers up and touched the tent walls, they were heavy with moisture, rain filling up all the pores, soon the wet would force its way through.

'Just close your eyes and get some sleep. The light will wake us early tomorrow.'

'OK,' his brother said. 'OK, James.'

He felt, sometimes, like Hiroji's father, as if the best part of his youth had already gone by. But these moments were fleeting. James was still only seventeen after all, he was just a kid.

It rained all night. Sometimes he heard voices floating through the schoolhouse, he heard trucks stalling in the mud outside. James knew they would come for him in the middle of the night, slash his throat and push his body into a pit before he was even alert enough to be afraid. He didn't want to die in the unthinking mud. He couldn't let this happen because there were people relying on him. There was Sorya and the promises he had made.

Kwan, this stranger, came to him in the shape of his brother and leaned his body against the far wall. His black hair fell forward over his eyes, his skin was the colour of cedar, he had thin lips and high, faint eyebrows. Every movement he made was precise, as if wasted movement itself was a crime, like spilled water in a time of drought. Kwan had Hiroji's watchful eyes. He was the opposite of James, he was not reckless or weak or self-pitying. Kwan took his time because he knew that the seconds were precious, doing the right thing in the right moment, every single time, was the only thing that could save him.

He studied Kwan and remembered his kid brother, the way Hiroji never spoke out of turn, never spoke without some prodding. If you didn't know him as James did, you would have thought that Hiroji was a bit slow, a bit dull, but really he was constantly rearranging things in his mind, he was opening and filing the information as it arrived, rather than letting it overflow and become meaningless. In the corner of the room, Hiroji, or was it Kwan or was it some metamorphosis of the two or was it James as he once was, the James that might have grown up in Tokyo with a father and a language of his own, with a box in his heart to hide his fear, shifted his weight and knelt on the ground so now they could see each other clearly, on the same level. The boy studied him. There was one man in this room and one ghost.

When James woke at the next knocking on the door, it was still pouring; rain was running thinly across the floor, cupping the light all to itself.

'Kwan?' the man's voice said.

James made no answer.

'Kwan?'

James reached out and plucked the weeds growing through cracks, he ate them and drank, foolishly, the dirty groundwater. Eventually, he heard the sound of the man's rubber sandals on the concrete landing, walking away. James's clothes were wet and they stank of the earth outdoors.

There's a room full of injured people and it brims with rot and excrement. The man leads James here in the middle of the night but what the hell is he supposed to do with no drugs, no nothing, barely even light to work by? He throws his hands up in frustration but the man doesn't seem to get it, he just watches expectantly as if James is Jesus with forty loaves at his beck and call. Forty ampoules. If James resists he'll get them all killed. He has no choice but to clean the wounds, dress them with scraps of cloth torn from the patients' own clothing, with wet cardboard or their filthy, multi-purpose *kramas*. He thinks about his brother, his mother, and no one seems to notice his tears.

Sometimes the patients are Khmer Rouge cadre and sometimes they are prisoners who are only being prepared for the next round of interrogation. Before, in Canada, he never wondered how many deaths one could survive, how many deaths one can bear, how many deaths one deserves. He doesn't know what to do with the children who have become as blank-eyed as the adults.

A blade of morning light falls in between the wall and the ceiling. The man, they call him Chorn, escorts James back to the storeroom. Before he leaves, the man orders a bowl of rice soup.

'Good night, Kwan,' Chorn says through the locked door. James doesn't answer. On the floor, beside his food, is a letter. It is a single, lined page torn from a notebook. He recognizes Sorya's handwriting long before he deciphers the Khmer words. The letter is bare of details. It is written to him. She must be here, in Cambodia, somewhere. She did not escape to Bangkok.

Sorya writes, *They told me you are safe. That you survived.*

When Chorn returns at nightfall, James says, 'What is this?' He has to control every word or they will overflow and hurt him. He says again, 'What is this?'

'I can bring you a letter now and then. This is all I can do.'

The words don't make sense to James. They don't tell him how the letter got here, or what it means. He picks up the sheet of paper, turns it over, looks for the information that is missing.

'Can you bring her?'

'That depends,' the man says.

James takes a breath and the fetid air sinks sharply into his lungs. 'You want to make every one of us small. Every one of us like you. Is that it?'

Chorn says nothing, he closes his eyes. He has a sharp face, a beak of a nose and long, dark lashes, he has an armoured quiet that nothing James understands can penetrate.

'Listen,' Chorn says. His voice is low and the words come so fast they seem to evaporate as soon as he speaks. 'Listen. I'm trying to help you. There is no other way. You want to know what we need from you? Everyone has to work. That's all. It's simple. There is no divide any longer between work and life, between life and death, between you and the world, between the world and Angkar. If you act correctly, you are the enemy, if you act incorrectly, you are the enemy. These are Angkar's own words. Can't you see that I'm trying to help you? A long time ago you were my friend. Don't you remember?'

James falters. He says, 'You can protect her.'

Chorn shakes his head. There's emotion on his face, like a mask that keeps slipping, that he pushes into place or removes at will. James is staring straight into his eyes and the man looks down.

'You still don't understand,' Chorn says. 'Unless you understand, we will both be accused. Not just her, but you and I as well. In Phnom Penh, you protected me. I never forgot.'

James tries to wipe the fog, the dust, from his thoughts.

'How did you get this letter? Explain it to me.'

'I have all the paper,' Chorn says, lifting his hands, opening his fingers. 'All the paper in this district, all the files, are here.'

Chorn touches James's shoulder and the shock of the gesture blinds him awake.

'She made a mistake,' Chorn says slowly, as if he is explaining himself to a child. 'Her letters to you are a crime. She should never have tried to reach you. But, now, it's too late to help her. She has been revealed to the authorities.'

James is not forced to work in the fields. He is not forced to do anything but wait. He hears a lot of things through the walls and what he hears is so chilling he believes, thought by thought, that he is a monster, that his mind is deforming. There was a woman in this prison. She was born in Phnom Penh but had gone away to study in France. She returned, a doctor also, to serve the country because she believed in the Khmer Rouge and a free Cambodia. The Khmer Rouge caught her in her home village, along with her family, and this woman was arrested and accused. After several days, she wrote her first confession, tortured into writing, claiming that she was a CIA spy. Tonight an ox-cart came and took her away to a different jail. James had helped prepare her for the journey and he saw her wounds, he saw the sadism of her interrogators, the ruptures on her skin. He wanted to tell her to succumb to her madness because madness is an escape, temporary or permanent, from this. From herself. But it was forbidden to exchange a word. He heard the ox-cart leave, turning up the earth, stuttering over the broken path, and the torturers laughing and saying their goodbyes. He saw this woman's face.

Sometimes, Chorn brings him outside, but only at night, only when all is still. A vitamin deficiency is causing his vision to blur so that when he looks up all the stars seem to be falling. Another letter comes a few weeks after the first, also delivered by Chorn. *I'm afraid,* she has written. *Every day I wonder if you will come. What should I do? They are watching me all the time.*

He asks for paper, for a pen. He begs for help.

'I am very sorry,' the man says. 'You cannot. It is far too dangerous.'

James feels his entire body sickening. 'Then you must tell her to stop writing.'

The man shakes his head, frustrated. 'Do you think it is up to me?'

'For God's sake, I'm begging you. Tell her to stop writing.'

They left him alone all day. This is when you lie in the water, when you lie down on the shore of the Pacific and the tide comes in and you have to let it take you. You have to go. You belong to no one, Angkar says, and no one belongs to you, not your mother or your child or the woman you would give your life for. Families are a disease of the past. The only creature under your care is you: your hands, your feet, the hair on your head, your voice. Attachment is what will expose you as a traitor to the revolution, to the change that is coming, that is here. Attachment to the world is a crime. For too long, the people have suffered. For too long they have waited, but their desire is as great as the sea, as thirsty as the dry land. Even the rivers are cruel.

He received another letter: *My love. They told me that you are near. They promised to bring you to me and I gave them all the money. I will keep trying to reach you, no matter the consequences. I want to bring about another future, the one I carried in my head for so long, all through the war.*

He started to weep and he couldn't stop. 'Help her,' James said. 'Hide her somewhere. Bring her here.'

Chorn looked at James. 'The truth is,' he said quietly, shamefully, 'there is no James. I have never known this person James.'

'Then tell her that he's dead. Tell her it's useless to write.'

Chorn removed a straw bag that was hanging from his shoulder, and from the bag he withdrew bandages, pills, antibiotics, brandy, dressings, even a stethoscope.

'All this suffering,' Chorn said, 'is for something. You don't know what this country was like before. You have to trust me.' The man held on to the supplies as if they were religious objects, promises.

He must be hallucinating. He rubbed his hands over the cement tiles. 'She didn't do anything wrong,' James said. 'I didn't do anything wrong.'

'Only a dictator or an idiot would make that claim,' Chorn said. He looked at the ground, at his toes protruding from his worn-down sandals, at the trail of dust he had brought into the already dusty room.

Chorn said in his quiet, detached way, 'Angkar knows about James. But it does not know about Kwan. You see how I have tried to help you? Because some of us have many tricks, some of us have many names. There are people who are loyal only to me, but even I know the limits of what is possible. Look at this,' he said, shaking the pills the way a mother might try to distract her baby. 'Look what I found. There is still so much that we can do. Everyone had a different life before but it doesn't mean we must all go to the same end.

'Would you find it hard to believe,' Chorn said, 'that once, long ago, I was a monk? They came to the temple and they took all the children away. They went and made us into something else.'

Before, when Dararith was still alive, they had taken the motorcycle to Kep and they had stayed a week on the seaside. The ocean comes into this storeroom and covers it like a drawing. He can see the tide taking morsels of the land, bit by bit, away. That week, Dararith had disappeared for three days – he'd met a French girl with long, waving hair, he'd offered to take her photograph with his brand-new Leica, but really it was Dararith who should've been the model. He was a handsome man with romantic eyes and full lips, and a mysterious, colonial sexiness that made the women foolish. In contrast, James was a bore, or at least that's what Sorya told him, teasingly, looking past him to the sea.

'And what about you?' he'd asked in English. 'If I wanted to take your picture?'

'I'm the true photographer,' she had answered in Khmer.

'Take your brother's camera, then.'

'I tried!' she said, laughing. 'Believe me, I tried. But Dararith, he uses it to meet women, it's only a toy for him, whereas I know I'm a photographer. If only someone would give me a chance.'

'What would you shoot?'

'Once I took a picture of my students at the Lycée.'

He never knew whether she was serious or joking. He was a buffoon, a hippopotamus, sitting beside her.

'I'm your friend, aren't I?' she had said on the last night that he saw her.

'Am I being demoted?'

'You're my best friend,' she had said, 'and you don't really know it. You don't value it.'

He'd felt belittled. He had wanted to raise his voice: I'm in love with you, is that such a small thing? I've loved you since the day I met you, why is that worth so little? Now he wonders how he misunderstood her so badly. How stupid, how arrogant was he, that he couldn't persuade her to leave for Bangkok; pride had made him unforgivably blind. He'd wanted her to wait for him. In his heart, he'd wanted this, to prove something, because they had both been alone. They had already left their families even before Angkar came. They only had each other.

'Tell me about Tokyo,' she had said, just like Hiroji. They were like two birds pecking at his head. On the southern borders of the city, rockets were falling. They could see the fighting, like sheaves of fire.

'There's nothing much to tell.'

'They bombed it very badly, didn't they?'

'It was Dante's fifth circle.'

'I used to teach that poem,' she said. 'I taught, "Through me is the way to the sorrowful city, through me is the way to the lost people."'

'Admit it, you have a lover somewhere, don't you?' he said lightly, wanting to turn the darkness aside. 'A boy much nicer than me.'

'I'm twenty-six years old,' she said. 'Everyone around me is married with ten children. I live in a city that's about to fall to the Khmer Rouge. What can I possibly know about love?'

'Come with me to Neak Luong. Come tomorrow.'

She shook her head.

'Take this money and buy us two tickets for Bangkok.'

'Honestly, you want to leave Phnom Penh? This heaven.'

'Do you?'

She smiled at him, she folded her sadness away. 'All this time, I only stayed because of you.'

The sea, the sea. The words ran in his mind, the future his father had once envisioned, the promises he had kept before he died.

'Some things don't end,' she said, kissing his lips. 'We both knew, didn't we? From the very beginning. I knew. You would be the one I loved.'

What did he say? He had only kissed her. He had treated everything as if it were ephemeral, as if things could only be beautiful if they were passing, if they were mortal.

'Can you hear me?' she had whispered one night, thinking he was asleep. He had kept his eyes closed. All those months, he had put on such a show of being brave, he made a joke of his needs. He had wanted to please her, to keep her, and he didn't know how.

He sleeps on the cement tiles, in the prison, segregated from everyone else because he is useful to Chorn. Sometimes the man comes and sits with him. Sometimes he brings a grandchild or a daughter and James gives them medicine, he cleans a wound, he works according to the tasks he is given. His own body is a parody of a human being, mere bones, dark shadows where muscle used to be. Kwan sits in the corner and day by day grows stronger, Kwan feeds memories to James, experiences that are part James, part Dararith and Sorya, part Hiroji, part Chorn. King James is a useless army of invisible men, of stories given and received like bread on the communion line, and it's the only bread he has to keep him going. King James is a rotten child, he's losing his mind and also his sight. Piece by piece, day by day, Kwan is taking over, and James is tired now, but he hangs on like a cat at the table because any scrap could be the one that saves him. He dreams of Sorya in the daytime, but never at night. Water seeps down the walls, along the green lines of invading grass, dribbling down to the ground.

Chorn goes away for many days, and a child, blind in one eye, brings the food. When Chorn returns, sick-looking, he asks James, 'Do you know anything about planting rice? About crops?'

James shakes his head. They sit quietly, and Chorn drums his fingertips against his knees. His hands are pale, as if, outdoors in the drenching sun, he keeps them safely hidden in his pockets.

'What's it like now?' James asks, breaking the stillness. 'In the cities.'

Chorn waits, without responding, without looking at James, as if Chorn, too, is expecting another person to answer. In the pause, there's the hard melody of an ox-bell, the only music James has heard in too long, and it seems to stretch like a physical object through the air and knock against the walls of the room.

'Everything is very organized,' Chorn says. 'They are making an archive in which nothing is missing. Every person must write a biography. They must write it many times to ensure that all the details are correct.'

He prays his hands together to stop the drumming. 'Phnom Penh is very still. In fact, it is empty. Every movement you make is like the first one ever made. I thought I was the only one alive. In the market, where the vendors used to be, there are small trees growing. Less than a year but already the jungle has arrived, it is threatening to strangle everything else.

'They have thousands and thousands of files. I delivered my share as well. I had to sign my name many times because they are terrified of missing pieces. Many times I signed my name.' Chorn runs his hand over his mouth, closes his eyes, and nods. James feels as cold as the walls. 'They put me in an apartment. A family's apartment. There were plates on the table, but the food had rotted. The owner collected stamps. Some were framed on the walls. I was standing there, looking at them, when the telephone rang. I went into the kitchen and the telephone kept ringing and ringing, I thought if I answered I would be punished, I was convinced it was a trap so I just stood there and waited, without moving, I waited for it to stop.

'Somebody's photos were sitting there, in the room, in picture frames. I don't know why, but I put one in my pocket. A photograph of a woman. She reminded me of my oldest sister. Do you remember her? You always thought she was pretty.'

Chorn looks up, an embarrassed half-smile on his lips. 'They are making an archive in which everything is accounted for, and once a file is there, it is eternal. This is Angkar's memory. We are all writing our histories for Angkar.'

Chorn pauses and in the gap, James says, 'What happened to your sister?'

He doesn't answer. Instead he says, 'Listen.'

The change happens so fast, James doesn't quite trust his eyes, Chorn's expressions come and go as quickly as a change in light. Chorn looks past him and James thinks that, finally, after all these months, he is about to be accused. Of what crime? It hardly matters. All the sentences are the same.

'This woman, Sorya. She had a child.'

Seconds go by but the words don't mean anything. It's a game, James thinks. It's yet another one of his sadistic games. They used to do this when they were young, tell each other stories. Once he ran home and told his mother that Hiroji had been hit by a car. He had wanted to test her, and he remembers now the strange satisfaction he took from the agony of her cries.

Chorn says, 'Maybe we're at the end now. There are purges everywhere. One hundred people, five hundred people. Soon we won't be alone, even here. The Centre is moving, you see. Angkar is running from itself, but it is meeting itself in every corner. Meeting all its enemies. Do you understand what I'm telling you? I have children too. I have children I want to save. I tried to find a name. Someone told me Dararith. I couldn't ask more without attracting attention. But they told me Sorya named the boy Dararith.'

The air in the room is stagnant, like a pool of black water into which they are both sinking. It's Kwan who finds the words, who asks the next question. It isn't James, James is falling down.

'Did you keep her here? Was Sorya at this prison?'

'No,' the man says.

'Was she here?'

Kwan gets up from the corner. He comes so near to them, James can hear him breathing, this exhalation in his head. Chorn is looking straight at him, but Chorn's face is closed, muting all the clues. Only his hands give him away, their immobility, their held breath. His hands are a lie. Was it possible that all this time his hands were a lie?

'You're my friend,' Chorn tells him. 'Why can't you understand? I'm giving you this information because you are my friend.'

'Why did they kill her?'

Chorn shakes his head, visibly upset. 'I don't know. Maybe she didn't die. Don't talk about this. Lower your voice.'

But then he reaches into his pocket and takes out Sorya's letters, five of them, creased and beginning to tear. He sets them on the floor and, for the first time, looks straight into James's eyes.

'Why are you doing this?' James says. He is nauseated and the man is breaking apart in his vision.

'Let her go. The past is done.'

The man stands up and dust comes off him, it sticks to the air.

James wonders why he doesn't stand up, push Chorn backwards, crack the weight of his skull against the cement wall, spill this man's life on to the once-elegant tiles, into the black water, go to be tortured and executed for a crime he can truly understand. His thoughts are viscous and slow. He could stand up now and find some strength, take this because there is nothing left to take. So what if Angkar is everywhere, he could kill this one man and be done with it here, he could choke his own weakness.

The door scrapes closed.

Days fall down, maybe it is a month that he sits like this, or just a few days, eating and sleeping and wasting away, remembering everything. Her watchful face, her scent, her hands pushing him back. No matter what the voice says, the animal won't move. There is water everywhere, he cries until all the rest comes out, all of it spills on to his ragged shirt, on to the tiled floor, and seeps into the cracks that lead out of the storeroom. There is no wind in this room, no oxygen. Where is emptiness? No matter where he goes, he can't find emptiness.

'Do you believe him?' Kwan asks.

James, wherever he is, trickling across the ground, spreading down to the lowest places, says no.

'No,' Kwan says. 'OK, James. OK. Let go.'

'I can't, I can't. I can hear her.'

'Don't listen.'

'I promised to bring her to the sea.'

'Let go, brother.'

'I promised her.'

'Let go.'

The last letter comes to him much later. He is standing at the Laos–Cambodia border and it is 1981, two years since the Khmer Rouge was defeated. In all that time, James, now known as Kwan – a mute, a smuggler, and a solitary man – has heard the most remarkable stories: the people who have been recovered, the strange ways in which children were protected, the objects returned to their owner's hands. He hears them at each and every encounter, when he trades the sugar and salt he has carried on his back from Thailand. The stories are repeated so often, they change into fairy tales of the most devastating kind.

In 1980, he went back to their apartment on Monivong Boulevard. There was a family living there, one of those new Cambodian families consisting of orphans: a man and woman with someone else's children, a friend turned uncle, a stray niece. They had traded everything of value in the apartment but they had held on to the photographs, without the frames, which they kept together in a blue plastic bag. Kwan gave them one precious US dollar and came away with photos of Sorya and Dararith, and of James. The stray niece came running after him and asked if she could keep the plastic bag, so now the photos stay in his shirt pocket, held to the fabric with a paper clip.

He went to Kampot, riding on the back of a moped driven by a ten-year-old who had stolen it from who knows where. This ten-year-old is so wizened he doesn't smile or laugh or anything. He just names, matter-of-factly, the price, US dollars or Thai baht, no other currency accepted. When the boy takes the cash in his bony fingers, he chews his lip and studies the bills, already assessing the things he has to buy. What a bombed-out ruin Kampot is now, buildings made unstable by the shelling, buildings that look as if someone kicked them in the kneecaps, hard. In his youth, Kwan drove a lorry so he knows these roads well, but still it's a shock to see the devastation and how the sea just keeps rolling in, unstoppable.

'Cigarettes,' the kid demands.

Kwan shakes his head.

'You can speak now,' the kid says abruptly. 'Angkar is done. Finished.'

Kwan gestures that he can't speak, he has never spoken.

The kid shrugs, folds the bills up, tucks them somewhere in his pants. 'My name's Joe,' he says, mangling the word. 'You need anything, you ask for Joe.' He revs the accelerator, the engine hacks, and he wobbles away over the cracked street.

That night, sitting on a mound of stones, he hears someone playing music on a record player. A man calls out the name Sorya and he lifts his head and sees a thin woman dancing slowly, her wrists turning in the same way they must have done decades ago, when she was a girl and this was Indochina and the French swanned down the wide boulevards and hid their guilt in a veil of opium smoke. Khmer dance is its own language, this is what Dararith had once explained: 'This gesture means you have come across a flower, a lotus, and you are offering it, and this gesture here means love. And this gesture is water.'

'Water, water, everywhere,' Sorya had said. 'Come and dance with me, Dararith. Nothing so classical. Just the *ramvong*. Just the lindy hop.'

'Wait,' Dararith had said. 'Let me take your photo.'

'Click away,' she said.

Here she is now, in his pocket.

He had felt, at the time, lonely: an outsider watching these two siblings, this self-sufficient love. But he knows now there are no outsiders. There is no walking away at the end, delusion has to finish somewhere, it has to end or else weakness will outlast them all. He has to commit to something or be done. From Kampot he travels to the prison where Chorn, too, was eventually arrested, eventually tortured and killed. In the storeroom where he passed nearly two years, boxes rot in the heat, files and pages, confusions, accusations. He went through them and found the sixth letter, the last one, the same thin weight of paper, but her handwriting had deteriorated, the pen had hardly any ink. Who was she writing to? Not James any more, or not just James. *They are throwing us away,* she wrote, *and I can't understand why because all I wanted was for the war to end, no matter who won. I never admitted any allegiance. My name is Sorya. I am the sister of Dararith, the daughter of Kravann and Mary, the wife of James. I was a teacher.* There was a biography and a confession, and in the biography was the name of their son, just as Chorn had told him. The prison file had dates, but no date of death, there was not even a photograph, nor was there a file for the baby, and he dared to believe that they had been absolved. That she wandered, like him, with a different name and a new soul.

'I'm a selfish Buddhist,' she had told him once. 'Something of me will return, something will come around and around forever, but it won't be Sorya. I have only this one chance.'

He travelled on, chasing a rumour of Dararith, to the Laos–Cambodia border where caves slip into one country and out the other. He, too, had hidden here for several months after running away from his work unit; they had been cutting trees in the forest when he attacked the lone cadre and left him for dead. Now he hardly remembers that he killed a boy. It is difficult to move during the rainy season. He can guess the date of his son's birthday. Small children, he knows, were sent to America, to France, they took flight to places he can't imagine, or they persevered, here, like Joe. They sold things or sometimes they sold themselves. The jungle has invaded the cities but now the hungry people are cutting it back. They are skinning the trees again and eating the bark. From place to place he defaces the walls with a black marker, Khmer words, Khmer letters: Sorya Dararith James. You can follow the trail but you can't know in which direction you are headed, down to the end, or reversing, forever, to the beginning. ■

THE
ANNIVERSARY

Nami Mun

After Jin-Ah got the call from the doctor's office, she gazed out of her living-room window. Thick clouds, black and hulking, stared back. It was mid-November, and drizzling. The low, grungy sky looked more like a wall than atmosphere. Even Will's favourite tree across the street seemed raw and thin, but little brown birds still whipped in and out of it as if it were spring. Jinny took this as a good sign. Only happy birds flitted about like that, she thought, and decided that she might also be happy. Then, just at that moment, a little brown bird, the size of a coin purse, flew straight into her window, making a crisp clunk.

Jinny shrieked.

She dropped the phone which she had forgotten to put down after the doctor's call. The battery pack and bits of plastic scattered across the wood floor. Damn it, she said to herself, and got to her knees, making sure not to move too suddenly for now a tiny something was starting inside her, dividing inside her. While putting the phone back together she couldn't help but laugh at herself for having shrieked when no one was around to hear it. If Will had been home, she wouldn't have made a sound. Will liked silence. He liked for the air to remain still. Sometimes they went entire evenings without talking and Jinny had simply grown accustomed to this.

She popped in the battery pack, scrunched in the wires. The baby, of course, would not be silent. Fearing Will's reaction, she considered telling him the news in public. Dinner at a restaurant, perhaps. A place with candles and circular booths of velvet. The idea cheered her up. The baby news would melt them back to love. Maybe they would sit side by side and hold hands, though they hadn't done so in a while, not even in private. She would look into his eyes, and if the moment felt soft enough, she would playfully hint at being pregnant by reciting a poem. 'I'm a riddle in nine syllables,' she would start, and after saying the final lines (*I've eaten a bag of green apples, boarded the train, there's no getting off*) she would make Will guess *what* she was, the way she made her AP English students guess. Will was a dentist, not a man of literature. He stared into mouths in search of disease. But he did enjoy puzzles and might like solving this riddle-poem. Jinny looked out of the windows again, the screens now jewelled with raindrops. They could take a cab to Lincoln Park and then, if time allowed, stroll to whichever restaurant caught their eye, light drizzles and grey skies be damned.

That was the plan, anyway. At six o'clock, Will did not enter the apartment, no matter how long Jinny stared at the door, willing him to. So she took a shower instead, listened for the deadbolt while she shampooed, and sprayed the tiles when she finished because the smell of bleach made her feel clean on the inside. Then came the nightly rituals. She separated her dirty underwear and bras from the rest of the laundry, creating a neat corner pile in the hamper the way Will preferred. She changed the sheets. She changed the blankets. In the living room she smoothed out the sofa, making it look as if no one had ever sat there, and then swiped a lint-roller across seats, and over pillows, picking up strands of her black hair and a few of Will's greys. Lastly, she turned on Will's computer in his home office, answered personal and school emails, and left the computer on sleep mode leaving her in-boxes open.

This only took her to 7 p.m.

Lesson planning on pathetic fallacies didn't work; she couldn't focus, so she watched the news. Weather forecast. Obama smiling. Palin smiling too much. At seven thirty, she refrained from looking out on to the street to see if she could spot him. He'll walk in when he walks in, she told herself, and then recited the poem three times, changed outfits twice, changed the water filter, and changed once more into a snug turtleneck and slim-fitting wool slacks, all of which erased only thirty minutes of her wait and none of her anxiety.

At eight thirty-five, when Will finally came in, she was by the door with her hat and umbrella in hand. She did not ask why he was late.

'What's all this?' Will began unbuttoning his coat.

'Leave it on,' she said, buttoning it back up. 'I thought we'd go out for dinner.'

'Jin . . .' He shrank away from her hands. 'I'm kind of tired,' he said, his voice small.

She looked at his chest. She couldn't convince her eyes to go any higher than that. 'A nice dinner might be good.'

'Maybe, but . . .' His hands completed his sentence as he took off his trench coat. He kissed her on the forehead, the pressure behind his lips as light as leaves, and walked into his office where he quietly but firmly slapped the rain off his coat before hanging it in his closet. Then, as he did most nights, he clicked on the lamp by his chair, eased into his cardigan – the same one he'd had since dental school – and opened *The Times* to the crossword puzzle, which he always completed with a pen. On nights when he made a beeline for his room as quickly as this, Jinny usually let him be until bedtime. But tonight, she watched him from the doorway, still holding her hat and umbrella.

'Everything OK?' she asked.

He didn't look up. 'Why wouldn't it be?'

Seconds later, he muttered, 'A long day, that's all,' and returned to his crossword.

Outside, the wind whipped the rain in too many directions. Telephone wires swayed and long arthritic branches scrawled on the windowpanes, the centre pane mirroring his lounge chair, the shrug in his posture, the slope of his nose. His soft brown hair, usually parted neatly to the side, was mussed and damp around the edges. His lips were pale. His eyes wide and at the moment murky behind water beads that clung to his glasses. The buttons on his cardigan were off by one, triggering something in Jinny's chest.

'Here.' She bent down to fix the buttons, smelling on him a mixture of rain and the oddly sweet tang of anaesthetic.

Turning his face to the side, he waited for her to finish.

'There,' she said.

He thanked her.

Jinny remained where she was and eyed the arm of his chair. As soon as he noticed, he slid over. She sat down. Her knee touched his thigh. Will moved again, giving her more room, and suddenly she felt between them an acre of distance. They hadn't been close, but they hadn't been this far apart either. The room was dark except for the yellow cone of light warming the paper's chequered squares. He'd gotten only two answers: the 'A' of 'atonal' linking with the 'A' of 'repast'.

'We haven't gone out in a while,' she said, as softly as possible.

He filled in more boxes, connecting words that had no right being together. As his pen scratched the paper, Jinny studied his long, thin hands. They sometimes seemed beautiful and dramatic. As if belonging to a mad concert pianist, or an impassioned sculptor chiselling away at the face of his mistress. Other times, like tonight, they seemed bony and starved – like hands excavated from a grave. Rigid blue veins travelled under his translucent skin, and under his wedding ring, sitting pale in the light. Their third anniversary was still months away. She wondered if they would celebrate. Without thinking, Jinny caressed the gold band. It felt smooth, and cold. Will paused, relaxed his hold on the paper and, after some silence, brushed his fingers over hers just as lightly.

'Where should we go?' he whispered, squeezing her hand.

The affair had happened in another city, in another state, nearly a year ago. And both had agreed never to speak of it. Sometimes, when Will travelled to a conference and Jinny was home alone, she would lie awake in bed for hours at night staring up at the ceiling, pretending that Will was the guilty one. The liar. The cheat. The sinner. In her mind, she's the one who sits in the kitchen, with the glass of untouched milk, not listening to the awkward grunts that echo through the house. She's the one who creaks the bedroom door open, still in her work clothes, and calmly asks Will to take a shower, and for the dark stranger to leave. And she's the one who makes him wash the sheets, smooth out the sofa, lint-brush strands of hair from every piece of furniture. These late-night imaginings lightened the weight of her body, sweetened the smell of her hair and skin. Sometimes she cried. Sometimes she masturbated. Mostly, during those hours of forgetting, she simply and happily lay with her innocence.

But she didn't think about any of this when they stepped out of their building that night. The baby news – that had to be her focus. It was dark, and the rain fell in fat glassy drops that ricocheted off parked cars. A puddle had collected by the front entrance, but Will push-buttoned his umbrella open, jumped over the puddle and crossed the street to stand under his favourite tree. Jinny, on the other hand, was stuck at the entryway, trying her best to shake open her umbrella. Will didn't notice. In his trench coat, and with all that water between them, he looked like the 1940s black-and-white image of the man who was always walking away at the end of the film. Disgusted, Jinny flung the useless umbrella into the lobby, shoved her hair into her hat and, with anger as momentum, she leaped over the puddle, better than expected. When she was about to cross the street, however, something dark, something she had seen, vaguely distracted her, enough for her to turn around.

It lay on its side, in the middle of the muddy pool; feathers wet and striated to the point of making the thing seem smaller than possible. It looked mangled, like something coughed up. Ignoring the water she now stood in, Jinny crouched down, and the details of the bird's injuries grew before her eyes. The beak was brown and barely hanging on his face. The eye a dull black seed.

'What are you doing?' Will waved her over. Jinny thought to shout back that she had known this bird, but even in her mind the words sounded ridiculous. She hated herself for having forgotten about the poor thing, for having spent her energy on putting the phone back together instead. And now she'd have to forget it once again so it wouldn't further smudge the night's already solemn mood. The baby was beginning. *They* were beginning. And a dead bird had no right to sully any of it. Jinny stood up, walked towards her husband and ripped the image of the bird in half, and then again, until its beak and feathers and bones were torn to shreds.

They walked down Broadway, a street wide enough for a plane to land. She wanted to hail a cab but Will insisted on taking the El, saying that the walk to the station would do them good. Headlights streaked by, buses honked at illegally parked taxis, and a police car zipped past, the siren sounding off-key in the rain. The air was a wet sponge. This was not the romantic stroll she had hoped for. The sidewalk was littered with soggy cigarette butts, old Obama signs and empty plastic bottles simply labelled 'Vodka'.

'The city should clean that up,' Will said.

'The bottles?'

'That too,' he said, speeding up his pace.

They passed cheque-cashing stores, gas stations and an abandoned chapel with plywood for windows. All the while, Will held the umbrella more over himself than her, and the right side of Jinny's face felt cold and pasty. She thought to speak up but then got sidetracked by a vacant taqueria they were now passing, and by the number of sleeping bodies piled inside its doorway. One man wore a plastic garbage bag like a poncho and slept sitting up, knees to chin. Another was shirtless. He lay on the cement in a foetal position, as if trying to crawl into himself.

'They must be freezing,' Jinny said.

'Who?'

'The men over there.'

Will looked back, and then straight ahead. 'This city's a dump,' he said bitterly. 'The country's falling apart.'

Jinny thought about the baby. 'I think things will get better.'

'Why? Because you say so?'

'I don't know . . .' Without making a big to-do, she slipped her hand into his coat pocket and laced her fingers between his. 'I'm glad we moved here.'

When he didn't respond, she added, 'I think I'm officially in love with Chicago.'

'Well . . .' He pulled out his hand to flip up his coat collar. 'We both know how easily you fall in love, don't we?'

His words numbed her face. She couldn't even look at him to see how much, if at all, he had meant to hurt her.

'Are you getting wet?' he asked, in a voice softer than she'd expected. He tilted the umbrella towards her a little. 'Where's yours?'

'I couldn't get it to work.'

With a finger he swiped at the mist on his glasses. 'I'll take a look at it when we get back.'

Jinny studied him – the sunken cheeks, the levelled jawline. He was right. Everything was reparable. Everything was salvageable. She remembered a story his mother had told her once. How when Will was in the first grade he'd won an award for frugality. He'd received the award because a teacher had seen him using a pencil the size of a matchstick. Will had sharpened both ends. When one end got dull, he would flip it over and use the other end. Jinny loved that story. He was the kid who played with one toy, the undergrad who worked two delivery jobs, the dentist who sometimes fixed his own equipment, and the husband who never threw away food, fading shoes, or old, gauzy sweaters, even when she'd begged him to.

The urge to hold him struck her, so much so that Jinny stopped walking. The rain was still rain but she didn't care. She just wanted Will to turn around and notice who and where she was.

'Jesus. What is it?' he said, the softness already gone. He stood maybe five paces away, under his umbrella, and didn't come for her.

'Nothing,' she said, moving her feet again.

At Argyle, they turned towards the El and walked into the smell of fish sauce and nail salons. In Little Saigon, restaurant windows displayed families hunched over their plates, their speedy chopsticks shuttling food into their mouths while the wait staff shouted orders, pushed along carts and served up what looked like bowls of steam. They reminded Jinny of her own parents who had come to the States with two hundred dollars and a dictionary. After slaving away in restaurants for over a decade, they'd eventually opened a hardware store which allowed them to work twelve hours a day, seven days a week, and come home smelling like keys. They were too tired to have affairs. Too busy to wonder if they were in or out of love.

By the time they reached the station and climbed the stairs to the elevated platform, it was a quarter past nine. They stood inside the waiting shelter, silent and alone. Jinny looked west, her back to the lake, and took in her view of Little Saigon. The sun had long set. The rain made puddles of restaurant rooftops and the night sky, now dark and wide, loomed above pink neon signs hawking noodles and tea. Against the windows of one restaurant, honey-glazed ducks hung by their necks, steaming the glass, until a man in an apron took one down, disturbing the line. The thwack of the cleaver smacked in her ears, the sound reminding her of the bird hitting her window. She again saw the muddy pool. The broken beak. The talons curled tight into a fist.

'Now that I'm partner, we can order the new ED4,' Will said, shaking his umbrella. The sound of his voice jolted her, in a good way she decided, so she answered quickly to act as though she'd been listening.

'That's good,' she said, and scrambled to remember what ED4 meant.

'Restorations will take less time.'

Equipment. It was dental equipment. 'I'm glad you and Charlie get along.'

'Yeah,' he said, looking directly at her. 'I finally get a good partner.'

Jinny's gaze fell to his shoulder, to his elbow, down to the tips of his scuffed-up shoes. She didn't understand his bitterness. He'd been distant but he'd never been mean.

'Maybe I can get that Subaru now,' he added, and she couldn't ignore his use of the first-person singular. The hard, spiteful expression on his face didn't match the casual delivery of his words, like a poorly dubbed film. The need to tell him the baby news felt immense at that moment. As immense as her need to hurt him back. He would feel guilty for every snide comment he had made today, she thought, and opened her lips to speak. To her surprise, he spoke first.

'I can't do this,' he said, his voice hollow.

'We can go back home if you want.'

'No. What I mean is . . .' He shook his head as if he couldn't believe what he was about to say. 'I have something to tell you.' His lips trembled, almost imperceptibly, just as they did sometimes when he slept. 'About tonight. I need to tell you why I was late.'

She looked down the long tracks. They seemed so endless, stretching for the horizon, following the curve of the earth. 'You don't have to,' she told him.

'I was across the street –'

'Don't you get it?' she said, not meaning to raise her voice. 'You don't have to say anything. You *never* have to say it.'

Will took off his glasses, wiped his eyes.

'Everything's fine,' Jinny told him. 'Everything's better than fine.'

Will let out a laugh.

'What's so funny?'

'You,' he whispered, putting his glasses back on. He stepped out of the shelter then and stared at the tracks. 'It's like I'm talking to a snow globe.'

Jinny knew too well what he felt at that moment – what it was like to want to confess, to have the words linger in your throat, only for them to get sucked back down. And she knew what he wanted to say. That he read her emails when she was at the market. That he sifted through her wallet while she slept. That he checked for hair on the bedding, on her sweaters, on the sofa – strands that weren't his or hers. That he smelled her clothes, her gloves, her dirty underwear. That he'd come home late tonight because he was standing across the street from their building, behind his tree, looking up at the rain and into their window to catch her, maybe, once again, in the act. That he did this more often than he admitted to himself.

She knew all of these things, she had always known. And after a while, she had come to take these rituals as a sign of his devotion, so she let him continue, helping him when she could by quietly performing rituals of her own.

'Do you even know what today is?' He was fixing the petals of the umbrella as if it mattered. 'An entire year, and I'm still looking for clues,' he said, and either laughed or sighed. 'Happy anniversary.'

Maybe she had known, and maybe not. She couldn't tell any more. She reached for his shoulder, wanting to offer some piece of herself, but he snatched her hand and gave it back to her as if to say it belonged on her body and not his.

A feeling, in the shape of an ice cube, became lodged in her throat. She wanted to break every bone in her hands. She closed her eyes briefly and imagined the right hand hammering the left, one finger at a time. The pain almost excited her. Down below, on the sidewalk, a little boy having a temper tantrum screamed and kicked as if someone was taking away his childhood instead of toy. She inserted the boy inside her chest and he kept screaming, in a pitch high enough to shatter every cell in her body as his mother dragged him by his ear down the block, crossing the alley. A car zoomed by, just missing the boy and his mother, and splashed gutter juice on to an old Asian woman carrying bags and bags of groceries that likely outweighed her. She cursed, her voice wavering up and down. And ignoring her cry was a young man in a bloodied white apron, walking past her, carrying an entire pig's carcass over one shoulder. The pig had been eviscerated, sliced down the middle, the skin a little crusty where he had been slit. Jinny's own chest loosened as she imagined being cut open from throat to pelvis, all of that wet confusion spilling out of her. Her baby would come into this, she thought, and looked to her husband who was now staring at the tracks, wanting to jump, or wanting her to.

The platform was quiet as the distant Red Line struggled towards them. Jinny didn't have to look. She could just feel it – a tiny rumbling under her feet.

'Train's coming.'

It didn't need to be said but she said it because she liked the certainty of it. The train was coming. She took a step closer to the platform's edge, and then another, until the cars screeched an inch from her chest and shattered all other sounds.

Bells rang. Doors opened.

Will went in without waiting for her. Jinny stayed where she was.

She imagined what would happen if she got on the train. *Your safety is important to us*, the recorded voice would say over the speakers, the tone sounding both robotic and concerned, as if he cared for her safety but only because he'd been programmed to do so. The way Will would sound if she told him about the baby. He would find a seat facing the wrong direction because he preferred travelling backwards, and she would sit by any window, so she could look out instead of in. They would pass Wilson and Belmont and the rain would warp her view of back porches, barbecue grills, old brick buildings made by old brick-hands, and a large billboard promising easy, speedy bankruptcy. And only then would she realize the word – the word she'd been feeling all day, maybe all year. Nothing was easy and nothing was speedy. Everything in her life – her baby, her marriage, herself – would sink slowly under water.

'Are you getting on?' Will asked.

She looked down the long platform. Other people with other lives stood waiting for the other train that travelled north instead of south. A young girl with doughnut-sized headphones swayed to her music. A man ate fish sticks from a bag, licking his fingers. And a big-bellied woman looked to the sky and said to her friend, 'Supposed to get worse tomorrow.'

'Are you getting on or not?' Will asked again.

She looked at him – his jaws locked tight, his eyes fixed on some box of bitterness set squarely in front of him. He's not done with me, she thought, counting out the metre and the stresses of the line. He's not done with me. ■

AGENDA
Poetry Competition

Hoofmarks Issue

Closing date 31 May 2011

Judges: Patricia McCarthy, editor of *Agenda*
       Sam Milne, sub-editor of *Agenda*

First prize: £1,000 Second prize: £200 Third prize: £100

The winning poems and the five runners-up (each of whom will receive a year's free subscription to *Agenda*) will be published in *Agenda*

Results: 31 July 2011

Rules:

1. The competition is open to anyone aged 16 or over.
2. Enter up to ten poems (£4 for the first poem, £3 for any additional poem).
3. Cheques and postal orders should be made out to 'Agenda'.
   No foreign currency can be accepted.
4. Each poem must be in English, no more than 45 lines, must not have been published elsewhere, and must be the original work of the author.
5. Each poem must be typed on one side of A4 paper, in single spacing.
6. The author's identification must not appear on the poem, but on a separate sheet of A4 paper with your name, address, email address and telephone number and the titles of poems submitted.
7. No online entries will be accepted.
8. No correspondence can be entered into and the judges' decision will be final.
9. The winners will be notified by post. No person may win more than one prize.
10. You can send in poems without the entry form.
11. All envelopes must be marked 'competition'.

Send your entries to: Agenda poetry competition,
The Wheelwrights, Fletching Street, Mayfield, East Sussex TN20 6TL

Alternatively, see what kind of poems we like:
SUBSCRIBE AND ENTER SIX POEMS FREE
1 year (4 issues = 1 volume): £26 (£22 OAPs and students)

Queries to editor@agendapoetry.co.uk   Details on www.agendapoetry.co.uk

INLAND, IRAN

Afshin Dehkordi

ONE DAY I WILL WRITE ABOUT THIS PLACE

Binyavanga Wainaina

I am home.

We sit in the dining room, and talk from breakfast to lunch, plates with congealing eggs littering the table. Every so often my mother will grab my hand and check my nails; a finger will reach into her mouth and emerge to lick a spot off my forehead, smooth my eyebrows. She stands to clear the table. She is swivelling her radar, like she used to do when we were children, half asleep, shuffling softly in her kaftan, disturbed by something intangible.

They are worried about me, and for the first time in my life, worried enough not to bring it up. I have not spoken to them about my stalled degree in a long time. They know. I know.

I am racked with guilt and am avoiding Baba. He has been gracious so far – has said nothing. All that wasted money on my degree.

I don't know how to explain my situation to them. I walk past the line of jacaranda trees that line government houses. I turn off the main road and follow the path, avoiding the path of Baba's morning drive to work. There is a small faded house here, right at the corner, with a large rocky garden that stretches downhill to border State House. It used to have a swimming pool – which is now grey and green and empty. It is one of several houses that were given to the children of Old Man Bomett, whose sister was married to the president.

There are stories about the rising jets of steam, that they are the ghosts of old Masai warriors trying to make their way to heaven, and being pulled back, by the gravity of hell. I heard them come in last night, the Masai *moran*, and their cattle. The strong smell of urine and dung flooded our house; and old throaty songs, and the cowbells. They sang the whole night, and for a while I could pretend that time had rolled back, and I sat among them, as a biblical nomad, or much as my great-grandparents would have.

I decide to spend some days travelling around, to avoid my parents, to follow a road and think about things other than what is wrong with my life. What a wonderful thing, I think, if it was possible to spend my life inhabiting the shapes and sounds and patterns of other people.

I have a part-time job. Driving around Central and Eastern Province, tasked with convincing farmers to start growing cotton again. I have been provided with a car and a driver. Baba and some friends have invested in an old government cotton ginnery which is being privatized. He asks me if I want to do some agricultural extension work for them. I say yes. They are starting to have some confidence in me. Up until now I have been helping my mother in her small florist's shop and running errands. I promised myself that I would not read any novels while sitting behind the counter. Sometimes I dash across to the club and sit on the toilet for half an hour with a book and a cigarette, but mostly I have been present in the world. Last week, at breakfast, I was expounding some theory or other, and Baba burst out: I don't understand, I don't understand, you are so intelligent, I don't understand why you are so . . . Mum sent a sharp warning to him across the table, and he stood up and left.

My colleague Kariuki and I are on the way to Mwingi town in a new, zippy Nissan pickup. The road to Masinga Dam is monotonous, and my mind has been taken over by the bubblegum music playing on the radio, chewing away, trying to digest a vacuum.

I donever reallywanna KillTheDragon . . .

It zips around my mind like some demented fly, always a bit too fast to catch and smash. I try to start a conversation, but Kariuki is not talkative. He sits hunched over the steering wheel of the car, his body tense, his face twisted into a grimace. When he isn't driving he is usually quite relaxed, but cars seem to bring out some demon in him.

To be honest, Mwingi is not a place I want to visit. It is a new district, semi-arid, and there is nothing there that I have heard is worth seeing or doing. Except eating goat. According to the unofficial National Goat Meat Quality Charts, Mwingi goat is second only to Siakago goat in flavour. I am told some enterprising fellow from

Texas started a goat ranch to service the 10,000 Kenyans living there. He is making a killing.

Over the years I spent living in South Africa, I drove past goats that stared at me with arrogance, chewing nonchalantly, and daring me to wield my knife.

It is payback time.

This is why we set out at six in the morning, in the hope that we will be through with all possible bureaucracies by midday, after which we can get down to drinking beer and eating lots and lots of goat.

I have invested in a few sachets of Andrews Liver Salts.

I doze, and the sun is shining by the time I wake. We are thirty kilometres from Mwingi town. There is a sign on one of the dusty roads that branches off the highway, a beautifully drawn picture of a skinny red bird and a notice with an arrow: Gruyere.

I am curious, and decide we should investigate. After all, I think to myself, it would be good to see what the Cotton Growing Situation is on the ground before going to the District Agricultural Office.

It takes us about twenty minutes on the dusty road to get to Gruyere. This part of Ukambani is dry, a landscape of hardy bushes and dust. Here, unlike most places in Kenya, people live far away from the roads, so one has the illusion that the area is sparsely populated. We are in a tiny village centre. Three shops on each side, and a large quadrangle of beaten-down dust in the middle on which three giant woodcarvings of giraffes sit, waiting for transport to the curio markets of Nairobi. There doesn't seem to be anybody about. We get out of the car and enter Gruyere, which turns out to be a pub.

It looks about as Swiss as anything could be in Ukambani. A simply built structure with a concrete floor and basic furnishings. I notice an ingenious drinks cooler: a little cavern worked into the cement floor, where beer and sodas are cooled in water. The owner walks in, wearing a *kikoi* and nothing else. His skin is sunburned tomato red. He welcomes us and I introduce myself and start to chat, but soon discover that he doesn't speak English or Kiswahili. He is Swiss, and speaks only French and Kamba. My French is rusty, but it manages to get me a cold beer, served by his wife. She has skin the colour of bitter chocolate and is beautiful in the way only Kamba women can be, with baby-soft skin, wide-apart eyes and an arrangement of features that seems permanently on the precipice of mischief.

When I ask her what brought her husband to Mwingi, she laughs. 'You know *mzungus* always have strange ideas! He is a *mKamba* now, he doesn't want anything to do with Europe.'

I can see a bicycle coming in the distance, an impossibly large man weaving his way towards us, his short legs pedalling furiously.

Enter the jolliest man I have ever seen, plump as a steaming mound of fresh *ugali*, glowing with bonhomie and wiping streams of sweat from his face. Gruyere's wife tells me he is the local chief. I stand up and greet him, then invite him to join us. He sits down and orders a round of beer.

'Ah! You can't be drinking tea here! This is a bar!'

He beams again, and I swear that somewhere a whole *shamba* of flowers is blooming. I try to glide into the subject of cotton, but it is brushed aside.

'So,' he says, 'you go to South Africa with my daughter? She's just sitting at home, can't get a job – Kambas make good wives, you know, you Kikuyu know nothing about having a good time.'

I can't deny that. He leans close, his eyes round as a full moon, and tells me a story about a retired major who lives nearby and has three young wives, who complain about his sexual demands. Parents in the neighbourhood are worried because their daughters are often seen batting their eyelids whenever he is about.

'You know,' he says, 'you Kikuyu can't think further than your next coin. You grow maize on every available inch of land and cover your sofas with plastic. Ha! Then, in bed! *Bwanaa!* Even sex is work! But Kambas are not lazy, we work hard, we fuck well, we play hard. So drink your beer!'

I decide to rescue the reputation of my community. I order a Tusker.

By eleven, there is a whole table of people, all of us glowing under the chief's beams of sunlight. My tongue has rediscovered its French and I chat with Monsieur Gruyere, who isn't very chatty. He seems to be under the spell of this place; as we drink, I can see his eyes running over everyone. He doesn't seem too interested in the substance of the conversation; he is held more by the mood.

It is midday when I finally excuse myself. We have to make our way to Mwingi. Kariuki is looking somewhat inebriated, and now the chief finally displays an interest in our mission.

'Cotton! Oh! You will need someone to take you around. *He!* You are bringing development back to Mwingi!' He volunteers to come with us.

We arrive at the District Agricultural Office. Our meeting there is blessedly brief, and we get all the information we want. The chief leads us through a maze of alleys to the best butchery/bar in town. He, of course, is well known here, and we get the VIP cubicle. Wielding his pot belly like a sexual magnet, he breaks up a table of young women, encouraging them to join us.

He whispers, in a conspiratorial aside: 'You bachelors must surely be starving for female company, seeing that you have gone a whole morning without any sex.'

Later, we head off to the butcher, who has racks and racks of headless goat carcasses. I am salivating already. We order four kilos of ribs and *mũtura*, blood sausage.

The *mũtura* is hot, spicy and rich; the ribs tender and full of herbal pungency.

After a couple of hours, I am starting to feel uncomfortable at the levels of pleasure around me. I want to go back to my cheap motel room, to settle into a book full of realism and stingy prose. Coetzee maybe? That will make me a Protestant again. Naipaul. Something mean-spirited and bracing.

No, no, no! says Mr Chief. You must come to my place, back to the village; we need to talk to people there about cotton. Surely you are not going to drive back after so many beers? Sleep at my house!

Back at the chief's house, I lie down under the shade of a tree in the garden, read the newspaper, and sleep.

Wake up! Let's go and party!
I am determined to refuse. But the beams from the old chief's face embrace me. By the time we have showered and attempted to make our grimy clothes respectable, it is dusk.

There is only space for two in the front of the pickup, so I am sitting in the back. I console myself with the view. Now that the glare of the sun is fading, all sorts of tiny hidden flowers of extravagant colour reveal themselves. As if, like the chief, they disdain the frugal humourlessness one expects is necessary to thrive in this dust bowl. We cross several dried riverbeds.

We travel so far away from the main road, I have no idea where we are. This lends the terrain around me a sudden immensity. The sun is the deep yellow of a free-range egg, on the verge of bleeding its yolk over the sky. The fall of day becomes a battle. Birds are working themselves into a frenzy, flying about feverishly, unbearably shrill.

I spend some time watching the chief through the back window. He hasn't stopped talking since we left. Kariuki is actually laughing.

It is dark when we get to the club. I can see a thatched roof and four or five cars. There is nothing else around. We are, it seems, in the middle of nowhere.

'It will be full tonight,' says the chief. 'Month end.'

Three hours later, I am coasting on a vast plateau of semi-sobriety that seems to have no end. The place is packed.

More hours later, I am standing in a line of people outside the club, a chorus of liquid glitter arcing high out, then down to the ground, then zipping close. The pliant nothingness of the huge night above us goads us to movement.

A well-known *dombolo* song starts, and a ripple of excitement overtakes the crowd. This communal goosebump wakes a rhythm in us, and we all get up to dance. A guy with a cast on one leg is using his crutch as a dancing aid, bouncing around like a string puppet.

The cars all have their interior lights on; inside, couples do what they do. The windows seem like eyes, glowing with excitement as they watch us onstage.

Everybody is doing the *dombolo*, a Congolese dance where your hips (and only your hips) are supposed to move like a ball bearing made of mercury. To do it right, you wiggle your pelvis from side to side while your upper body remains as casual as if you were lunching with Nelson Mandela.

I have struggled to get this dance right for years. I just can't get my hips to roll in circles like they should. Until tonight. The booze is helping, I think. I have decided to imagine that I have an itch deep in my bum, and I have to scratch it without using my hands, or rubbing against anything.

My body finds a rhythmic map quickly and I build my movements to fluency, before letting my limbs improvise. Everybody is doing this, a solo thing – yet we are bound, like one creature, in one rhythm.

Any *dombolo* song has this section where, having reached a small peak of hip-wiggling frenzy, the music stops and one is supposed to pull one's hips to the side and pause, in anticipation of an explosion of music faster and more frenzied than before. When this happens, you are supposed to stretch out your arms and do some complicated kung-fu manoeuvres. Or keep the hips rolling, and slowly make your way down to your haunches, then work yourself back up. If you watch a well-endowed woman doing this, you will understand why skinny women are not popular among many in East Africa.

I join a group of people who are talking politics, sitting around a large fire outside, huddled together to find warmth and life under a sagging hammock of night mass. A couple of them are students at university; there is a doctor who lives in Mwingi town.

If every journey has a moment of magic, this is mine. Anything seems possible. In the dark like this, everything we say seems free of consequence, the music is rich, and our bodies are lent a brotherhood by the light of the fire. Politics makes way for life. For these few hours, it is as if we are all old friends, comfortable with each other's dents and frictions. We talk, bringing the oddities of our backgrounds to this shared place.

The places and people we talk about are rendered exotic and distant this night.

Warufaga . . . Burnt Forest . . . Mtito Andei . . . Makutano . . . Mile Saba . . . Mua Hills . . . Gilgil . . . Sultan Hamud . . . Siakago . . . Kutus . . . Maili-Kumi . . . The wizard in Kangundo who owns a shop and likes to buy people's toenails; the hill, somewhere in Ukambani, where things slide uphill; thirteen-year-old girls who swarm around bars like this one, selling their bodies to send money home, or to take care of their babies; the billionaire Kamba politician who was cursed for stealing money, and whose balls swell up whenever he visits his constituency; a strange insect in Turkana that climbs up your warm urine as you piss, and does thorny unthinkable things to your urethra.

Painful things are shed like sweat. Somebody confesses that he spent time in prison in Mwea. He talks about his relief at getting out before all the springs of his body were worn out. We hear about the prison guard who got Aids, and deliberately infected many inmates with the disease before dying.

Kariuki reveals himself. We hear how he prefers to work away from his family because he can't stand seeing his children at home without school fees; how, though he had a diploma in agriculture, he has been taking casual driving jobs for ten years. We hear how worthless his coffee farm has become. He starts to laugh when he tells us how he lived with a woman for a year in Kibera, afraid to contact his family because he had no money to provide. The woman owned property; she fed him and kept him in liquor while he lived there. We laugh and enjoy our misfortunes, for we are real in the group, and cannot succumb to chaos today.

Kariuki's wife found him by putting an announcement on national radio. His son had died. We are silent for a moment digesting this. Then somebody grabs Kariuki's hand and takes him to the dance floor.

We talk and dance and talk and dance, not thinking how strange we will be to each other when the sun is up in the sky, and trees suddenly have thorns, and around us a vast horizon of possible problems will re-establish our defences.

The edges of the sky start to fray, a glowing mauve invasion. I can see shadows outside the gate, couples headed to the fields.

There is a guy lying on the grass, obviously in agony, his stomach taut as a drum. He is sweating badly. I close my eyes and see the horns of the goat that he had been eating trying to force themselves through his sweat glands. It is clear – so clear. All this time, without writing one word, I have been reading novels and watching people, and writing what I see in my head, finding shapes for reality by making them into stories. This is all I have done, forever, done it so much, so satisfyingly; I have never used a pen. Maybe – I am not just failing; maybe there is something I have that I can barter, if only for the approval of those I respect. I have lived off the certainty of others; have become a kind of parasite.

Self-pity music comes on. Kenny Rogers, *A Town Like Alice*, Dolly Parton. I try to get Kariuki and the chief to leave, but they are stuck in an embrace, howling to the music and swimming in sentiment.

Then a song comes on that makes me insist that we are leaving.

Sometime in the 1980s, a Kenyan university professor recorded a song that was an enormous hit. It could best be described as a multiplicity of yodels celebrating the Wedding Vow.

Will you take me (spoken, not sung)
To be your law- (yodel) *-ful wedded wife*
To love, to cherish and to (yodel)
(Then a gradually more hysterical yodel): *Yieeeeei-yeeeeei -MEN!*
Then just Amens and more yodels.

All these proud warriors, pillars of the community, are at this moment singing in unison with the music, hugging themselves (beer bottles under armpits) and looking sorrowful.

Soon, the beds in this motel will be creaking, as some of these men forget self-pity and look for a lost youth in the bodies of young girls. I am afraid. If I write, and fail at it, I cannot see what else I can do. Maybe I will write and people will roll their eyes, because I will talk about thirst, and thirst is something people know already, and what I see are only bad shapes that mean nothing. ■

Beyond the Crash: Overcoming the First Crisis of Globalisation *Gordon Brown*

The international financial crisis holds our global economy in its grip. In *Beyond the Crash*, former Prime Minister and Chancellor of the Exchequer Gordon Brown writes his extraordinary account of how the situation occurred and his view on what the global community must do next in order to climb out of the abyss.

Simon & Schuster £20 | HB

The Tiger's Wife *Téa Obreht*

Set in a Balkan country still scarred by war, *The Tiger's Wife* is the haunting, transcendental debut novel of Téa Obreht, the youngest author on the *New Yorker*'s Top 20 Writers under 40 list and one of the youngest authors ever to be extracted in the magazine. She has been described by Colum McCann as the 'most thrilling literary discovery in years'. This is one to watch.

Weidenfeld & Nicolson £12.99 | HB

Red Dust Road *Jackie Kay*

From the moment when, as a little girl, Jackie Kay realizes that her skin is a different colour from that of her beloved mum and dad, to the tracing and finding of her birth parents, her Highland mother and Nigerian father, Jackie Kay's journey in *Red Dust Road* is one of unexpected twists, turns and deep emotions. A compassionate, life-affirming and extraordinarily moving memoir.

Picador

Index on Censorship

International in outlook, outspoken in comment, award-winning magazine *Index on Censorship* is the only publication dedicated to freedom of expression. In the current issue, read Margaret Atwood, Tom Stoppard and Ngũgĩ wa Thiong'o on standing up for their fellow writers in the name of free speech. The issue is produced in association with English PEN.

Subscribe to the magazine online for £18 a year, or in print for £28
Single copies of the new issue are available for £7.99
Visit www.indexoncensorship.org/subscribe

Darwin's Bastards: Astounding Tales from Tomorrow edited by Zsuzsi Gartner

Social satire, fabulist tales and darkly humorous dystopian visions make up these 23 stories. William Gibson, Yann Martel, Sheila Heti and Douglas Coupland, among many, take us on a wild ride into future times and parallel universes where characters as diverse as a one-legged international actuarial forensics specialist, a pharmaceutical guinea pig, and a far-sighted foetus engage in their own games of the survival of the fittest. **Douglas & McIntyre $21.95 CAN, $16.95 US**

PU-239 and Other Russian Fantasies
Ken Kalfus

In these seven unforgettable, comic, and hair-raising stories, Kalfus moves effortlessly through a century of Russian history. 'There are funny, hip writers, and there are smart, technically innovative writers, and there are wise, moving, and profound writers. Kalfus is all these at once' (David Foster Wallace). 'Kalfus is an ironist in the best late-modern Central European style: wry, humane, precise, and beautifully smitten with ideas' (Jonathan Franzen). **Milkweed Editions $16**

The Hottest Dishes of the Tartar Cuisine
Alina Bronsky Translated by Tim Mohr

Europa celebrates its 100th title with this edgy and wry take on warped family dynamics from the author of *Broken Glass Park* (2010). 'Alina Bronsky writes with a gritty authenticity and unputdownable propulsion' (*Vogue*). In this dazzling new novel, the Russian-born author trains her prodigious talent on Rosa, the world's most munificent and selfless grandmother, and her innumerable hapless victims. **Europa Editions $15**

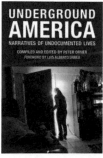

Underground America: Narratives of Undocumented Lives
edited by Peter Orner; foreword by Luis Albert Urrea

Millions of immigrants risk deportation and imprisonment by living in the U.S. without legal status. They are living underground, with little protection from exploitation at the hands of human smugglers, employers, or law enforcement. *Underground America*, presents the remarkable oral histories of men and women struggling to carve a life for themselves in the U.S. **McSweeney's, $16**

ENGLISH HOURS: NOTHING PERSONAL

Paul Theroux

It is the happy, often pompous delusion of the alien that he or she is a witness to an era of significant change. I understand this as a necessary conceit, a survival skill that helps to make the stranger watchful. I lived in England for eighteen years, as a pure spectator, from the end of 1971 until the beginning of 1990. I was just an onlooker, gaping at public events that did not involve me. I was a taxpayer but couldn't vote; a house owner, but still needed an entry visa; and for quite a while I had to carry an Alien Identity Card.

Having lived for six years in Africa and three in Singapore, I knew how to be an alien. Keep your head down and stay current; save all documents and receipts; take nothing for granted. You are not owed anything. 'Nothing personal' is the alien's motto, because the alien has no security, and no discernible future. I had a family, a wife and small children to protect: I was anxious. 'You Yanks,' people sometimes said to me, when they heard my accent, as though I needed to be reminded I was an alien. But an alien is reminding himself of that every moment in the foreign country. The alien has to practise cunning to disguise this twitchy state of mind; but insecurity stretches the nerves, heightens the attention and makes the alien remember. Mine wasn't an era; it was simply eighteen years of events. For an alien, life in the foreign country, never completely comprehensible, is always eventful.

Early on, it was a period dominated by smoking. The top deck of the bus was a designated smoking area, people chain-smoked in doctors' waiting rooms, British Airways allowed pipe smoking at the back of the plane, many movie theatres had smoking sections: an era of blue smoke and fruity coughing. The craze for bar billiards and snooker crested in the 1970s, with a surge of interest in snooker on TV, a show called *Pot Black*. The single-screen cinemas began to be transformed into bingo halls. Later, when cinemas became scarcer, churches were deconsecrated and gutted so that they could serve secular purposes, bingo among them. This surprised me, and I was shocked when Christian churches were turned into mosques.

Public events dominated my attention, as they do all aliens looking for ways to fathom the foreign country and their own slender connection. The stories unfolded – the Yorkshire Ripper, the miners' strike and the three-day week when a shoe-mender in Sydenham refused to serve me; he pushed me out the door (it was his day to close early, to save coal, to subdue the miners). A plane crash in the spring of 1972, the aircraft dropping like a stone into Surrey, and the emergency vehicles unable to get to the scene, because so many people on this sunny Sunday drove to see the carnage (118 people killed), blocking the narrow roads with their cars.

The deaths in Northern Ireland were always in the news, the bombings all over. Bloody Sunday occurred about two months after I arrived: fourteen Irish protesters gunned down by British soldiers, and many wounded. 'The Paras know what they're doing,' was the line up at the Gollop Arms in South Bowood, 'and one of those dead blokes had a nail bomb in his pocket.'

Bombs, bombs! So many of them on lovely days, in parks and public houses, on Christmas Day, in hotels, nearly all of them the work of the IRA, whom I saw as aliens, like me. Even the car park of the House of Commons was a bombsite, the MP Airey Neave, about to be named Northern Ireland Secretary, blown up in his car. The Guildford pub bombing of '74, four people killed, many injured, and the same year, in two pubs in Birmingham, twenty-one people murdered. Lord Mountbatten and three others, including two children, blown up on his yacht, *The Shadow V*, while on an August holiday in Ireland. To the mournful echo of the bomb, came the sententious crowing, the toothy triumph of Gerry Adams, cock-a-hoop with the deaths on the yacht.

The official IRA line was always, 'Look what you made us do! It's your own fault!' A large nail bomb in '82 in Hyde Park killed four soldiers and seven horses; another the same day, a large bomb under the bandstand at Regent's Park, instantly killed seven of the bandsmen and seriously injured all the rest, plus many people in the audience – another sunny day, the band playing selections from the musical *Oliver!*. Six people killed at Harrods in '83, at Christmas time. A bomb at three in the morning at the Grand Hotel in Brighton that was intended to kill Prime Minister Thatcher and her whole Cabinet – five people killed, many injured. Thatcher, working on her speech at the time, survived.

There were much worse bombings in Ulster, just as cowardly, just as vicious, just as pointless. IRA member Bobby Sands went on a hunger strike, demanding prisoners' rights in Long Kesh Prison, where he was serving fourteen years. Refusing food, he intended to call attention to his list of demands: 'The right not to wear a prison uniform,' and others. He wished, punishing himself, to arouse pity. But the IRA bombs were in everyone's mind. And, not understanding that most people didn't care, and certainly not the prison staff, probably glad to see him suffer, Sands died of self-imposed starvation.

The clearest memory I have of the whole nasty Ulster mess, of cruelty and bloody-mindedness, is a newspaper picture of a skinny teenaged Irish girl whose boyfriend was a British soldier: tarred and feathered, gleaming black, with white tufts stuck to her body, her head shaven, terrified, pushed along a street by a howling mob of Catholics. She looked like an alien to me, suffering the alien's fate of rejection – in her case, extreme and humiliating.

It was years before anyone dared openly to mock the royal family. The Queen, with her hint of spiritual authority – Defender of the Faith – was spoken of in whispers. 'She works jolly hard,' was the mantra. Princess Anne was named Sportswoman of the Year in 1971. I wondered, was the princess in her show jumping an inspiration to the footballers on the council estates?

One night a man named Fagan climbed the wall of Buckingham Palace and broke into the Queen's bedroom. Unable to summon help, Her Royal Highness sat with Fagan, in her dressing gown, until she was finally spotted and Fagan taken into custody. But he couldn't be charged with breaking and entering – it wasn't a criminal offence. So, Fagan was found guilty of stealing a bottle of the royal wine and at his trial when the subject of the Queen came up, he grew indignant and said, 'I won't have that woman's name dragged through the mud!' or words to that effect.

Prince Charles got ostentatiously married and appeared in an iconic pose with Diana on a postage stamp; Prince Andrew's marriage to Sarah Ferguson was memorialized with a special label on a bottle of cheap champagne, at about the same time it was revealed that Sarah's father frequented a certain massage parlour, the Wigmore Club, for a weekly wank.

Wank was a new word for me. I learned others in those years: pantechnicon, pastilles, salopettes, anorak, ginger wine, trifle, syllabub, riddling (the coal grate), gaiters, trug. Secateurs, borstal, Boche, Gorbals, yobboes, scotia (a sort of household trim), valance, shandy, sent to Coventry, applied for the Chiltern Hundreds, chicane (as of a set of racing cars), gauntlets, whitebait, infra dig, subfusc, knackers, Christmas crackers, Dutch courage, Dutch cap, double Dutch, Screaming Lord Sutch.

I watched the conductor on the 29 bus on Lavender Hill making change, working his ticket machine with two hands and holding the money in his mouth, biting on the pound note. When I stumbled he quipped, 'Have a good trip!' and the other passengers hooted. The estate agent in Clapham explained that the five-bedroom house on the market for £10,000 had no central heating, 'Just arm-swinging.' Denis Healey said in a speech, 'You're out of your tiny Chinese mind.' George Brown demanded to be in the House of Lords, because he had just turned fifty-three, had worked hard enough in his political life, and he needed a sinecure. He didn't seem very old to me, but he got his sinecure and became drunken, idle Lord George Brown.

Another Labour lord, George Wigg, Baron Wigg – he had enormous ears – was arrested for 'kerb-crawling', another new expression to me. He denied it and was acquitted; but it was apparently true. It was known that he stalked strolling prostitutes in his car. He was a mate of the prime minister, Harold Wilson, who had ennobled one crook after another, Lord Kagan, Lord Miller, and others. Those were Labour men. Jeffrey Archer, a similar piece of work, who claimed to be head of the Conservative Party, became Baron Archer of Weston-super-Mare: another crook, a proven liar, slimy, with a history of fiddling funny money schemes, and now a lord. So this was how the system worked!

A news item that struck me – this was in the 1970s – described a woman who was charged with trying to encourage her mother to commit suicide, so that she could inherit the house. 'Mummy, take the pills,' and the mother sweetly replying, 'I'm not sure I want to, love.' The daughter persisted, 'Go on, Mummy,' and almost succeeded, until the mother's nerve failed her, and the plot fell apart.

Sir Anthony Blunt, the Queen's adviser on paintings, expert on Poussin, turned out to be a Soviet spy, and a traitor. This fascinated me: here was an intelligent and well-connected Englishman, authentically horse-faced, who (so it seemed to me) had set out to make himself an alien. But Blunt was living proof that such a man could not succeed in becoming an alien, even in his treachery. He held a grand position; he was exposed; he did not fall far. He had betrayed many people, but still had many friends, and his connoisseurship was widely respected. He was asked how he felt about being a traitor. 'Dreadful,' he said languidly, in the tone of an afterthought, as though he was talking about having a bad cold. He summed up for me another way British society worked. He hardly suffered, was never put on trial, still had his chums and defenders; it was a victory for suavity, and after he was unmasked he wrote his *Guide to Baroque Rome*.

No one knew much about the SAS, even the initials themselves were obscure, until 1980, when the Iranian Embassy in London was taken over by Iranian separatists. Hostage negotiations continued;

London was watching. Then, black-suited soldiers abseiled into the building from helicopters, killing all the hostage-takers except one. 'You let one of the bastards live,' Denis Thatcher said, smiling, to one of the SAS men at the award ceremony afterwards.

The killing of the police officer Yvonne Fletcher never left my mind. It was in the spring of 1984; she was patrolling a crowd of protesters outside the Libyan Embassy in St James's Square. And then she fell, killed by a bullet from a gun aimed by someone inside the embassy. And when the embassy was closed not long afterwards, and the diplomats swaggered out to the square – to fly home to Libya – the TV announcer said, 'One of these men killed Yvonne Fletcher.'

Of the many scandals, each contained a memorable line. 'Bunnies can and will go to France.' Jeremy Thorpe, leader of the Liberal Party, had written to a man who was said to be his former lover. He was entangled with this male prostitute yet denied everything and got off. The man in question, Norman Scott, had been targeted by one Gino Newton, who shot his dog Rinka but failed to kill Scott. Scott revealed love letters from Thorpe with the 'Bunnies' quote. It turned out that Thorpe might have been involved in the plot to murder Scott. But Newton was no genius, confusing Dunstable with Barnstaple. The judge lowered his head and said to him: 'Even a moron in a hurry would know the difference.'

'Lie doggo.' The Lord Lucan scandal. Lucan, in an attempt to kill his wife, by mistake bashes in the head of his nanny Sandra Rivett. The name Rivett was always repeated with a smile (like the name Olive Smelt, whom the Yorkshire Ripper had attacked). Lucan tried and failed to kill his wife who ran from the house covered in blood, to the Plumbers Arms in Belgravia, screaming, 'Help me!' Later, Lucan wrote in a letter to his friend Bill Shand Kydd: 'I will lie doggo for a while.'

'If you stay here much longer you will go home with slitty eyes,' Prince Philip said to some British students in China in 1986.

'*Gotcha!*' was the *Sun* headline when 323 Argentine sailors died in their ship, the *General Belgrano*, days after the beginning of the Falklands War. The Argentines struck back with missiles. 'It's like two bald men fighting over a comb,' the poet Borges said in Buenos Aires. And before this unnecessary war was over, with the capture of South Georgia, Margaret Thatcher hooted in triumph, exhorting the country with the single word: 'Rejoice.'

After Idi Amin expelled the Indians from Uganda in the early 1970s, they began to run the corner shops, the newsagents, off-licences; the shops were kept open later and later – unprecedented hours. I identified with the Indians as fellow aliens and sometimes spoke Swahili to the newsagent on St John's Hill, from Tanzania, who missed the place terribly. We drank in the Fishmonger's Arms, an Irish pub, and he would frown into his beer and say, 'It's mango season,' meaning in his home town of Mwanza, on Lake Victoria.

These Indians knew everything about being aliens: they had lived as outsiders in East Africa and had great survival skills and a kind of accommodating and contemptuous deference. They began to take over the failing sub-post offices, the bill paying, the parcel weighing, the banking, the albums of postage stamps: none had run post offices in Uganda, but some had been *duka-wallahs*, shopkeepers, and could handle complex paperwork, the smudgy pads of carbon paper. They were willing to work on weekends, or on early-closing days. But the post office was shrinking – it had begun to shrink in the first decade of my residence.

No one seemed to notice, or care, though it was an inconvenience to me when the Sunday-evening pickup at the mailboxes ended. I worked during the week on my own books, but on weekends I usually did a book review. I read the book on Saturday, wrote the review on Sunday and always posted it that evening so that it would be on the editor's desk the next day. The Royal Mail was a good name for this efficient system. As the years passed the post offices contracted; and then they became like toy shops, selling sweets and knick-knacks and no one got their mail on time.

England does not have a climate; it has weather, seldom dramatic. So I was astonished when the worst windstorm since 1703 hit the south of England one dark early morning in October 1987, killing eighteen people. I was woken by my own burglar alarm, and the racket of many other nearby alarms. I had no lights; big branches had fallen from the sycamore tree in my back garden. I called Battersea Police Station, and though the phone was promptly answered, the policewoman could not help me. She said that everyone had the same problem: 'It's the wind.' When I asked for more information she said, 'I am sitting in darkness.' In the grey light of dawn I went out and saw the plane trees down on Wandsworth Common and across side roads. A man walked towards me, animated by the chaos, smiling, excited, blurting out to me, a complete stranger, 'I've just come from Clapham Common. It's worse there! Trees all over!'

Of the many riots, in Belfast and Derry, in Liverpool, Notting Hill, Brixton, Clapham Junction and elsewhere, the riot that scared me most was not any of the ones that erupted near my home. Many times I had seen vandalism and riot damage, broken and boarded-up windows just down the road in Clapham Junction; I was even becoming used to observing sudden mayhem, football hooligans, racial incidents, windows casually smashed and cars broken into in south London.

But the riot in October 1985, in Tottenham, north London, on Broadwater Farm Estate, made me wonder. A howling mob, intent on destruction, chased and hacked to death an isolated policeman. This was Police Constable Keith Blakelock, overwhelmed by screaming masked rioters, wielding knives, and when they got him down they used these knives to try to behead him. They found that a human neck with all its bones and muscles and tendons is a hard thing to sever; and these maddened murderers failed, though they sawed at the flesh and bone for a long time, hoping for a trophy.

What I remember best was Bernie Grant, the unapologetic local councilman, weighing in. He was about my age, black, born in Guyana. He had been an alien once, but was now an accepted political hack with a following. I was fascinated by his confident smile, by his saying that the police had asked for trouble, and, 'What the police got was a bloody good hiding.' He did not mention that the fallen policeman, covered in blood, his face smashed, killed by the crowd, had been partly decapitated. I understand that a municipal building in Tottenham has been named in his honour – not Keith Blakelock, but Bernie Grant; an arts centre.

These public events gave me a greater detachment, a growing sense of not belonging. I always listened for clues. On the radio, the line-up of panellists on *Any Questions?* sometimes indicated what the prevailing opinions were for or against the issues. They talked about TV shows. *The Family*, a BBC series that was broadcast in 1974. Terry and Margaret Wilkins and their family, a big vulgar shouting bunch, had allowed cameras to film all their comings and goings – one of the earliest of what now would be called a reality show.

'I tell my children that they are lucky that we live in a happy home,' one of the *Any Questions?* panellists, journalist Jacky Gillott said, when asked about the propriety of the show. She described how dysfunctional this TV family was. 'Not all families are like the Wilkinses.' She seemed sure of her family, but one night about five years later, Jacky Gillott went upstairs, and with her children still in the house, she killed herself.

And then there were the silly movies, the awful music, the bad art, the sports failures, all the defeats, the public cheats, the liars, the nine-day wonders, the stars – Simon Dee, Dusty Springfield, Erica Roe, Russell Harty, the talked-about actors of *Coronation Street*, in *Crossroads* and *The Archers*, all of them described in Dr Johnson's trajectory: 'They mount, they shine, evaporate and fall.'

The bombs were the worst, for the awful deaths and for the way they changed the texture of life. It is so easy to be a bomber or a sniper in a civilized country. And the dreary results were metal detectors in unlikely places – museums, for example; and bag searches; and the left-luggage facility was rendered too dangerous to continue. It got so that any briefcase in a pub looked like a bomb.

The sleazy aristocrats and the crooked politicians, the spies and the trimmers, seemed to taint the whole society. Jeffrey Archer's books were stacked and sold everywhere, and they always seemed to me a visible sign of corruption. The horrible man wouldn't shut up, wouldn't go away. And though an apology from any of these creepy people might not have undone any of their crimes, it would have been something, a gesture. But in a society where 'Sorry!' was almost a catchphrase, on most people's lips, no one who should have ever said sorry did – not Wilson, nor Archer, nor Blunt, nor Major Ferguson, nor Bernie Grant, nor Gerry Adams, none of them. 'Sorry' was never uttered by one of the biggest crooks of the lot, Robert Maxwell, a certified alien – born Jan Ludvik Hoch in Carpathian Ruthenia. He had changed his name, got a British passport, become a Member of Parliament, a schemer in publishing, an insider in the Labour Party, and a greedy embezzler. Cornered in his crookery, he killed himself by jumping from his luxury yacht off the Canary Islands. No suicide note; no regret. Regret was perhaps implied in the last act of Harold Wilson's crooked friend, Sir Eric Miller – a Jew – when he killed himself on the Day of Atonement. But it wasn't an English thing; it seemed an alien gesture.

I endured the horrible unapologetic faces in this national farce, until the action became repetitive, or incomprehensible, or frightening, or frustrating. Some of the people I knew were awarded knighthoods or went into the Royal Academy, or the House of Lords; half a dozen killed themselves, or got rich, or vanished. Many of my writer friends ended up in the United States, participants in my culture, as I never was in theirs in England. 'Nothing personal,' I said to myself. As an alien, I was living in a house that just happened to be in England. I never stopped writing: it was my mode of being. And then one day, knowing there was no place for me here, I slipped out, as some aliens do, and never came back. ■

HERE IS WHAT YOU DO

Chris Dennis

You wet your hair in the sink, then comb it back, slick as a new trash bag. You look nice. OK, so your name is Ricky. You are twenty-three years old. People say you're sweet. You say to them, 'No, I'm not.' But you are. You know you are. You can't help it. It's like there's a piece of candy hidden deep inside you and everyone is trying to find the easiest way to get it out.

Your cellmate, Donald Budke, he's like Rasputin, or Genghis Khan, maybe even Napoleon Bonaparte. No one tells Donald he's sweet. His motives are serious, and he's got acne scars which make him look like a criminal. He is a criminal. He's ten years older than you, is on his fourth year of a fifteen-year sentence for manslaughter. You're just a high-school history teacher from southern Indiana, or at least you used to be.

On the day you were arrested, the US customs agent said, 'What the hell are you doing, Ricky?' like he knew you or something, like he was really disappointed. 'Who's the vehicle registered to, Ricky?' You told him it was your grandmother's. You gave him your driver's licence, your car keys. He asked you to sit in the back of his patrol car while he searched your trunk. You watched through the windshield, waiting for him to find the five cottage-cheese containers full of oxycodone you'd hidden beneath the spare tyre. The sky was pink, like a drop of blood in a glass of water. You thought, Mexico is like an art film. You thought about the ten or so pills in the pocket of your pants, wished there was some way of keeping them so you could eat them later, in the event you were placed under arrest. You didn't want to eat any of them right then. You were already as high as a butterfly. You fished the handful out of your jeans pocket and put two in your mouth anyway, waited for the spit to come, swallowed. The rest you chewed into a paste and spat on to the floorboard of the patrol car while the customs agent rifled through your roadside emergency kit.

The man came back and said, 'You need to step out of the car,

Ricky.' You stood beside the highway while families in minivans drove by, the early-evening heat like needles pricking your face.

Before the customs agent put you back in the car, he said, 'Anything else hidden on your person becomes a felony inside the jail. Is there anything else, Ricky?' You stared at his ears, which were so big and red. They suited him, you thought.

'No, sir,' you said. 'Where else would I put it?'

'Never mind,' he said, looking away.

You could hardly hold your eyes open.

Hours later inside the customs office, another man – not much older than you, his eyes pale as pool water – told you to relax your hand while he rolled your fingers across an ink pad, pressing the fingertips on to a little index card with your name on it. The fingerprinting station was fascinating, and you told him so. You talked to him about Henry Faulds, a squat man, you said, who wore funny hats, credited with being the first person to use fingerprints for identification. 'He used a greasy print left on a bottle of alcohol,' you said.

'Well, all right then,' the man said.

He put you in a small room by yourself, a concrete cell with puce-green walls and no windows. You lay down on a metal bench that was bolted to the floor. You drifted in and out of the thing the pills made you feel. You thought about Horatio Nelson and the final moments in the battle of Cape Saint Vincent – the fleets falling out of formation on the water, gun smoke rising towards the sails, Nelson reaching out to take the surrendering sword of San Jose. You slept, turning constantly on the hard bench, shaking the whole time from nervousness and the thought of never going home and the thought of not having any more pills to take. The lights went off, and then later came back on again. A man opened the door to say you could use the phone. You followed him into the racket of the booking office and called your nanny.

'Good afternoon,' Nanny said when she answered the phone. You tried to explain about the pills but she kept saying, 'Ricky, how did this happen? Should I come get you?' When you said you were in Texas she started to cry. That wasn't the worst part.

'Who's done this to you? Should I call the police?' she asked. There was a loud crash on the other end of the phone, something breaking.

'What was that, Nanny?'

'I dropped a plate of food. Where's the car, Ricky?'

'I'm being arrested, Nanny. I have the car. I'll bring it back.' And you meant it, without even realizing you wouldn't be able to. She said she'd call the secretary at Woodrow Wilson High School to tell them you wouldn't be at work on Monday. She told you not to worry about the dogs, she'd find someone else to walk them. This made you feel deserted, and damned. Nanny didn't get it. 'Can the neighbours do it?' you asked. Nanny said she had to go, to clean up the food. 'Nanny! Nanny!' you said, after she hung up. The officer next to you reached for his Taser. You dropped to the floor and hid your face. 'Jesus,' he said, before helping you up.

After two weeks in the Webb County Jail, Judge Henry Travers of the eleventh circuit court sentenced you to one year at Lewis Prison in Woodville, Texas. 'You'll only serve four months,' your public defender said afterwards.

You spent eight days in a holding cell with a car thief named Teddy from Houston, then down a long, loud hall full of men yelling and watching as the guard took you to your room. Donald was sitting on the edge of the bunk reading. The guard handed you your toiletries. The door made a shocking click-clicking noise when it closed. Donald moved his hair out of his eyes, held out his hand for you to shake.

'You like Tom Clancy?' Donald said, showing you the cover of his book.

Most of the cells here are two-man rooms with bunk beds, like the one you're in. There are three dormitories with around seventy men in each and people get moved all of the time but you've been in the two-man cell with Donald since your intake. Everywhere you turn there are black men. They huddle in the dorms, or else move through the block like schools of shimmering fish spotted by the rare scrawl of a white face. When the white men smile, their slim mouths are filled with rotten teeth. At first there is a lot of crying and vomiting and shaking, coming off the beautiful pain pills you'd grown, over the past year and a half, to love enormously. This is prison. Donald says he can't find you pills in here and that anyone who can is looking for a hook-up. Sometimes the old dudes will offer something boring at the canteen, Effexor or Ambien. These do not help.

You look at yourself a lot in the mirror. You're lanky – bony and gaunt. Your hair is too blond, the cut pathetically neat. Everyone in here seems taller than you. Even the shortest felon seems like a giant.

Donald tells you that some of the other inmates have offered him money for the chance to get at you. 'What do you mean?' you ask.

'What do you call a blond with half a brain?' he asks.

Two months in and already you are ashamed of so many things, things you had no idea a person could be ashamed of. One, for being educated, because most of the men here never made it through high school. You feel embarrassed around them, like Louis XVI must have felt after his arrest, surrounded by the working class in the Temple Prison – not condescending but humiliated.

Your cell has a toilet with a sink attached. The sink is attached to the top of the toilet where you think the tank should be. At first this made you uncomfortable about washing your hands. You're used to it now. You have to straddle the toilet facing the tank or stand to the side of it when you brush your teeth, or wash, or get a drink. You push a button above the faucet and the water comes.

The recreation room reminds you of the teachers' lounge at Woodrow Wilson High. One of the dudes in there, he can hardly read the newspaper. When you first saw him, sitting with the paper open, sounding out the words to himself, you thought you'd help him. He was skipping the words he couldn't figure out. You went over and pulled up a chair. 'Can I have a look?' you said. This was before you knew how things worked.

He said, 'Get your own fucking paper.'

'It's *nay*-bourhood,' you told him, 'not *neeg*-bourhood.'

'I got it,' he said, sliding his chair away. 'Now get the fuck off me you faggoty fuck.'

'Sorry,' you said.

Your lip was trembling. You couldn't think of anything good to say. You got up and went to the other side of the room. You sat in one of the yellow vinyl lounge chairs next to the window pretending to read *People* magazine. You sit there a lot now. You try not to make eye contact with anyone you suspect might be illiterate.

You told Donald the story and he laughed. You pretended to laugh too, but also you were crying a little. You didn't let Donald know.

Donald has long black hair. Many tattoos. His teeth aren't perfect, but you've seen worse. There is something dim and monumental in his eyes – the irises grey as tombstones. He grew up in Iowa. You can hear it when he talks. He calls cola 'pop', and other things like that. This is not the only reason you like Donald but it has a lot to do with it. He says he's in for manslaughter, but he won't say anything else. You ask him what happened but instead he talks about his hair. 'There were a few guys in here that used to fuck with me,' he says, 'because I wouldn't cut my hair and because sometimes I put it up in a ponytail. They used to say to me, "What's under the ponytail, Donald, a horse's ass?" All I have to do now is give them the look.'

He stands up really fast, like something bad has just happened. You're not sure what's going on. He gets right up in front of you like he's considering the quickest way to crack open your face. 'That's what I do,' he says. 'That's the look I give them.' He starts laughing. 'Works, don't it?'

You nod. Your pulse knocks inside your ears. 'It does. For real.'

He says now he tells them to shut the fuck up and they shut the fuck up. You're sure you're not capable of this.

'Try it,' he says.

'I don't think so. I'll just be cool. I'll stay out of their way or else give them my dessert at dinner.'

Donald points his finger at you. 'Shut the fuck up!' he yells. He makes a fist, brings it up to your mouth and presses the knuckles against your lips. 'Stop fucking talking right now!'

'Why? What did I do wrong?' you say into his knuckles.

'No, Ricky. Damn it. That's what you're supposed to say to them. I'm not telling you to shut the fuck up. Shit, dude, you've got to stop being such a giant pussy.' Donald shakes his head, like he can't believe people like you exist. 'I'm trying to help you,' he says. 'You're going to be in here a really long time. You've got to at least try.'

You've been here two months now. 'Yeah,' you say, 'two more months.'

'You'll be lucky if they ever let you out,' Donald says. He picks up his book. *Without Remorse* it's called, and it must be serious because Donald will sometimes talk aloud while he's reading, usually to cuss out the bad guys who he says are always corrupt cops. He lies down on the bed holding the book open in front of his face. 'It's gonna suck without you here, man.'

You've been with him almost every hour of every day since you got here and you're still not sure what to do when he says these things.

He lays the book down on his chest. He says, 'Some dudes make friends in here and then get all depressed if they leave. You're lucky I'm not like that. I'd never try to kill myself or anything.' He picks up the book again. 'I'm reading now, don't talk to me.' He stares at it, turns a page. 'Bitch,' he says, and then, 'Just kidding.'

Another thing you feel ashamed for is Donald. You can't remember ever thinking of a man in this way. You had a girlfriend for a while in college, Janice Pickett. You looked at her and you liked what you saw. She was short, breasts like half-filled water balloons, strawberry-blonde hair. On the old couch in your dorm room, spring of sophomore year, she took your virginity. She took off your clothes and sat on your lap. There was a sudden wetness on you, like maybe she'd just spilled warm soup on your penis. You made an awkward groan and came inside her. She got up and ran to the bathroom. After that you went on dates together to the movies and to sports bars. You bought flavoured condoms and laid a blanket down on the dorm-room floor, thought about important moments of the American Civil

War and tried not to come as soon as she climbed on top of you. You liked her, thought about asking if she wanted to move in together. Right before graduation she showed up saying, 'Let's keep in touch, Ricky. Sound good?' But it sounded awful, like she was making fun of you or something. That was two years ago. You haven't had a woman since. The female teachers at Woodrow Wilson made you nervous when they started acting sexy, cornering you in front of the faculty microwave. You just never thought about guys. One time in college a drunk guy at a house party showed his penis to everyone in the room. It made your face hot, caused a tingling feeling in your stomach, but you didn't want to touch it or anything. Why would you? You only thought it looked weird. It was big.

When you find out that Nanny reported the car stolen, her car, which you drove from Indiana to Mexico to the buy the pills, you aren't angry exactly, just frustrated. Frustrated is a better word for it. Nanny forgets things. She can't help it.

She can't come to visit but you call her on Thursdays. At first she only asked about the car, kept telling you that someone had stolen it. 'Can you believe someone would do that to me?' she said. Two months in and she's finally stopped with that. Instead she tells you she hopes you're doing well, that she's proud of you, and proud of your new job in Pittsburgh, where she says you're teaching history again. She says you should go and straighten up the desks before class every day, pick up all the little bits of paper trash off the floor so that the Lord can come into a nice clean classroom before each session, inspiring the children to learn and truly love their lessons. 'Will you do that for me, Ricky? Will you try it and see if it makes a difference?'

'Yes,' you say, 'I'll do that, for sure, what a good idea.' Then you walk back down the hall, through all the loud and mechanical doors towards your cell, where Donald is playing rummy against himself or watching *The Maury Povich Show*. 'How was it?' he says.

'Oh, it was whack,' you tell him.

At 9 p.m. the lights and the television are shut off. Sometimes it takes a while for the cell block to quiet down. The other inmates are always laughing or yelling. Eventually one of the guards calls for everyone to knock it off. Donald has the bottom bunk, and he usually waits fifteen or so minutes before he asks if you're asleep. You say, 'No, I'm still awake,' and then Donald asks if you want to come down there.

'Whatever,' you say.

You'd been in here maybe a month when Donald first said it, and now after a few weeks of it, you just climb down from your bunk and try not to look nervous. You wait for him to make a spot for you next to the wall. You lie stiff as a book against the cold concrete and wait. You both lie there for a minute without touching until he asks if you want to suck. That's when the tingling in your stomach starts. If you want to suck you put your hand on his penis, which is already so hard that it sticks up out of his underwear, flat against his stomach under the tight elastic of his briefs. You play with it for a minute before putting your face under the covers. Sometimes he asks if you'd rather fuck, in which case you roll over and face the wall. It's nothing, really. Just a heavy weight. A heat in your joints. A current travelling. This is what cellmates do.

About the pills. You had an abscessed tooth, right – a cavity and then a pain like a wide throb across your face that woke you up one morning before work. Your dentist – the same one Nanny had been taking you to since you were little – scolded you for letting it get that bad, prescribed ten days' worth of antibiotics and twenty Vicodin, told you to come back in a week and a half. The first pain pill made you dizzy and tired. You slept straight through the night. The second one made you vomit. The third one lit a glorious fire in your head that eventually spread to your chest and arms and groin until it had invaded your whole body. Everything was right in the world. Nanny was a thin, white angel mixing vanilla pudding at the kitchen table. The children at school were blurs of pink and green with flesh tones in between. Instead of reading aloud from the textbook every day you wrote lectures for the first time. History books became the things they used to be on sunnier days alone in your old dorm room. The surge of

those sagas opened up to you like ancient mausoleums.
You read:
The Life of Wilhelm Conrad Röntgen.
The Sephardim in the Ottoman Empire.
A History of the American Privateers During Our War with England in the years 1812, '13 and '14. You could put your hand over your eyes and see battlefields, crowded infirmaries, the torch-lit corridors of Nubian pyramids.

After that you were making appointments at the doctor's office all the time, complaining of back pain, neck pain, chronic headaches, a burning sensation in your kneecaps. You'd take Lortab, Vicodin, Percocet, Percodan, Tylox. It was like learning a secret language. Some of the pills were more exciting than others. You saw three different doctors, had prescriptions filled at every drugstore in town, until finally Shirley Lynn Dobbs at Dobbs' Drugstore started asking questions, making calls.

It was maybe a week later that you saw the article about pharmaceuticals and drug laws in *Newsweek* – they mentioned Mexico, speedy clinics in the backs of grocery stores and novelty shops, prescriptions for anything a patient was willing to pay for in cash. You thought of nineteenth-century China, of the thriving opium trade and those covert smoking divans. It sounded like the most perfect retreat.

It was the Thanksgiving holiday. You told Nanny you were going to Indianapolis to hear a seminar on the Miami Indians of the Midwest. You emptied your savings, cashed in a couple of bonds. You had enough pills to last three days. You got in Nanny's car and drove. And drove. And drove. The sun and the moon came and went.

The day before Thanksgiving, in Nuevo Laredo, you rented a room at the Red Roof Inn. You got lost two days in a row, ate too many cheap enchiladas, asked the wrong people the wrong questions in the wrong language until you finally decided that the back-door pharmacies were made up, were more like small invisible cities of El Dorado than the luxurious opium dens of China.

On the last night, at the Chaser Lounge, you let Kenny Voglar from Carson City, Nevada, buy you too many strawberry margaritas. Kenny wore a lime-green tank top and a diamond ring. He claimed he was once the president of the Rod Stewart fan club. He had a soft spot for GHB and Xanax. He said he knew a man who had exactly what you were looking for. You could see your reflection in the mirror behind the bar. The Christmas lights strung around the alcohol bottles made little flashes of colour across your face like so many blue and red stars blinking off and on.

The man who had exactly what you were looking for was actually a seventeen-year-old Mexican kid in short-shorts with a Madonna tattoo. Kenny talked. The Mexican kid turned up 'Like a Prayer' on the stereo and danced. Kenny watched. You stood by the door, pretending to read the ingredients on a package of gum. After the song was over the kid went into the bathroom, made some noise, brought out five cottage-cheese containers full of pills. He handed you one of the pills. You took it, and sat on the floor watching the Hispanic boy and Kenny Voglar snort something off the bedside table. They danced around to the music while you waited for the pill to do its stuff. After twenty minutes or so you decided you maybe liked Madonna. 'Vogue' seemed like an interesting song. The Hispanic kid did a special dance for it. He seemed very talented. You gave him all of your money. He gave you all of his cottage-cheese containers.

If you don't answer Donald when he asks if you're asleep, he says, 'I see how it is. What? You mad at me? You got a problem, Ricky?' But you're never mad at him. You're just worried. You lie in your bed and fake the loud, steady breaths of deep sleep. You feel the bed start to shake, Donald furiously taking care of himself on the bunk beneath. He's only touched your penis once, wrapped his hand around it and squeezed for a second. After he finishes in your mouth or on your back he quickly pulls up his pants and rolls over and you climb up to your bunk.

Once, after he was finished fucking, you started to get up and he said, 'Don't move.' He put his arms around you, pressed his face into your back, touched you neatly on the spine with his nose. You might have stayed like that all night except Donald woke you up later, smacking you in the head, saying, 'Go back to your own bed, faggot.' An inmate a couple cells down was yelling, 'It's my stomach. I think it's the pancreas! I need a doctor!'

'Shut the hell up,' someone else yelled.

'No shit,' Donald called back, 'because you don't even know what a pancreas is!'

You met with your drug counsellor for the first time and he told you your official release date. May 14. It is now the fifth of April. He said he was proud of you, which was odd since you'd only met with him once. Still, it was nice to hear. You asked when you would have to appear before the parole board. He said, 'This is a kind of parole hearing right now. You've done everything right. Good job, Ricky.'

You come back into the cell and tell Donald that things went great with the counsellor. Donald is sitting on the floor, shuffling the cards. 'Where's *Rainbow Six*?'

'Where's what?'

'My new Clancy book, idiot. Where the fuck is it?'

'I haven't seen it.'

Donald holds up the deck of cards with one hand, presses them between his thumb and index finger so that the cards go flying. There's something in his mouth. He looks up at you while the cards fly. He spits hard across the room, hitting you, perfectly, on the mouth. He says, 'Don't think you're better than anyone else in here! You fucking drug addict. If you get out you'll be back on drugs in no time. Then you'll be dead.'

You stand with his spit running down your chin. You want to say something but the spit clings. You don't wipe it away. Just stare at the wall with your mouth closed tight. You think about the Korean War. Think about President Harry S. Truman or picture old Douglas MacArthur standing on the grassy banks of the Nakdong River polishing his sunglasses with a handkerchief. Wait for Donald to look away and then use your shirtsleeve to wipe away the spit. You go and put your mouth under the spigot. You wonder how much tobacco it must have taken General MacArthur to fill his gigantic pipe. Think about your counsellor. Think: Good job, Ricky. Good job.

Nanny is your mother, or she might as well be. There has never been anyone else, at least not that you can remember. You remember a day years ago, before the pills, right after you moved home from college. You were in the living room with Nanny. The dogs, Ashley and Lyle, were asleep under the coffee table, their noses at Nanny's feet. She sat her Dr Pepper down on the china saucer she used for a coaster. You loved the sound it made after each drink, when she returned the can to the saucer, the warbled ping of aluminium to china. 'You know, honey, to me Dr Pepper tastes like vanilla extract. And you know what else? I think you have always been this way. You have always been like you are now, even as a little boy. A criminal mind, some people call it, but I think you could be a minister. Your great-grandfather was insane. He used to choke rabbits to death in the shed. He enjoyed it. You remind me of him.' You were flattered, even though it was clearly one of her less coherent days and you weren't entirely sure what she meant. She kept calling you Larry, who was maybe an old friend of hers. She'd go through a short list of names – her grandfather, distant cousins – before she called you by the right one. It made you proud to know you reminded her of a dangerous person. You only wished you were the sort of person who could choke a bunny. You wonder if Nanny somehow knew this was coming.

The day after Donald spat in your face the two of you sit on the floor and play spades as if none of it happened. Donald has a tattoo of a black knife surrounded by a spiral of thorns directly over his Adam's apple. You stare at his throat, not at the tattoo, but at the thick apex of bone there. It reminds you of something. A pill. A tree. An erection.

'One time I choked a rabbit to death,' you tell him.

'My lawyer fucked me over, really did a number on me,' he says.

'What do you mean?'

'Just did, man. Just did.'

This isn't good enough. You want the history. The timeline of events. You want the body count. But before you can ask him, Donald reaches into his pants and takes out an oatmeal cookie. 'I saved it from lunch. It's all yours.' It's against the rules to leave the mainline with food, and you don't like oatmeal cookies. But you eat it anyway. Donald says, 'Ricky, I was trying to help you. That's why I spit on you. Every motherfucker in here is going to try and spit in your face, or worse. They don't give a shit whether you live or die. You're not free yet, man. You're still an inmate. I just want you to be prepared. I just really care about you. I take care of me and mine.'

During the last few weeks you keep your hands clean. Shave every day. When you shower, you always use more soap on the parts of you Donald pays most attention to: hands, butt, hands.

Nanny sends many cards. The last one: *Life is well in Pike County. Ashley is eight! Lyle has been injured! Those crazy people down the street with the camouflage golf cart! Ashley whines at your bedroom door. Lyle always thought so much of you. You didn't forget about him, did you? He would always follow you around when you killed the flies so he could eat up the dead ones! Went to lunch at Long John Silver's with my sister. She's been coming over to walk the dogs. I might get tired of her soon! Been thinking of you. Been thinking of you so much. Submitted your name to the prayer chain at church.*

Climb into bed. Get back up. Read the last chapter in all of Donald's books. Write a letter to Nanny. Drink water from the sink. Wet your hair. Comb it straight back. Look at yourself in the metal of the sink and think: *Not bad, Ricky.*

You like the black guys but sometimes they throw pieces of food at each other during dinner. They make a mess. They ask you what you're looking at and you offer them your fruit cup. One of them comes and takes it. 'Thank you,' he says. Apparently he doesn't like the pear chunks, because he spends the rest of the time throwing them back at you every time the guard looks away. Finally Donald comes in and sits down, sees the pear chunks on the table, a piece stuck to the front of your jumpsuit. He looks over at the black dudes but they're looking at their food, pushing it around with their spoons. 'What the fuck?' Donald says. Eventually someone lifts their head. Donald points at him, picks up some of the pear, throws it and hits him right on the forehead. They both stand up.

'Fuck no,' Donald says. 'Sit right back down.' When the guy doesn't sit down, you say to Donald, 'Don't. Just forget about it. I don't care about the pears,' but Donald is walking over with his tray in his hands and breaking it over the guy's head. One swift crack against the man's face and the guards are dragging Donald out of the mainline. You're just standing there, not saying a word, with fruit still stuck on your jumpsuit.

Donald's skin is tan and tough from years of working in the sun. He was a labourer. He roofed hotels in Cleveland, worked as a garbage man in Louisville, did other things in Chicago. 'You go where the work is,' he always says.

He is gone for over a week. In solitary confinement. You can only wonder what is happening to him. Sometimes men will spend months in the hole. No television. No books. No one to talk to. Donald came on you the night before he hit the guy in the face with the food tray. You don't take a bath while he's gone. You keep the smell on you. Put your hands on your back, between your legs, up to your nose. It is the smell of something old, something unclean and sour and terribly personal. This is what it's like with him.

Several inmates approach you in the yard. They enclose you, dark and scary as a basement. They want to know if you're looking for anything. One of them gets right up in your face. He says, 'You're fair game now that your dude is gone.' He tells you, 'This way, buddy. Walk over here.' But one of the senior guards, Clint maybe, or Gary, comes and stands between the two of you. He says, 'Come on, Ricky. That's enough. Let's go.' He takes you through the gymnasium, and all the way back to your cell. 'You need to get your shit together,' he says. He wants to know how a kid like you ended up in Woodville.

'Drugs,' you tell him.

He laughs at that. 'What else,' he says. It's not a question.

You lie in bed the rest of the time smelling yourself and thinking about Donald: how he only sleeps on his back; how the blood pools in the sink after he brushes his teeth; how he always cleans under his fingernails with an envelope, how his semen tastes, how it sprays over you in varying arcs – the distance it goes, the sheer and warm amount of it shooting across your body.

When he finally comes back you're in the recreation room sitting in your chair by the window, reading a magazine. You watch him walk in. He's freshly shaven. His hair is pulled back, combed and wet. You're not sure if you should smile. You know you pay too much attention to him in front of other people. He stands on the other side of the room talking to some of the other men from your block. He looks so clean, just back from the showers. You're still dirty. You walk over and stand next to him. You don't speak. It takes him a minute. 'What's up?' he says, like he hardly knows you. You have to keep your hands tucked into your waistband to keep from reaching out and stroking his ponytail. Here you are, like Hephaestion standing in the court of Alexander the Great, pretending to listen to the strategies but instead thinking of how he's going to make you feel after the troops disperse.

When you're both back in the cell Donald says, 'They'll put someone else in here as soon as you're gone. I wonder who it will be? I hope they're cool.'

You imagine another man in the cell. You imagine the lights going out, the room quiet for a few minutes before Donald asks this other man if he's asleep. You wonder what Donald means by 'cool'.

At lights out you take all of your clothes off and wait for him to ask you. After maybe half an hour has passed and he hasn't said anything you climb down and get into his bed. For the first time, you kiss him. Maybe you shouldn't but you want to try.

'What the hell?' he says, jerking back, like he doesn't understand. 'I'm not your fucking boyfriend.' He grabs your head, pushes you down towards his crotch. 'Do me a favour,' he says.

For the rest of the week, after lights out, Donald says nothing or else he just comes up to your bunk. He says, 'Turn over.' He presses his fist against the small of your back and whispers in your ear. He says, 'You like it now, don't you? You love it. You want me to own it.' He says, 'You like it when it hurts?'

You tell him you like it when it hurts. You tell him you want him to own you.

You talk to Nanny on the phone. You tell her you need a way to get back to Indiana. You tell her the car was impounded, you don't have the car, she'll have to pick it up.

Nanny is upset. 'Ricky, you've got a good job there in Pittsburgh. It's a friendly city. I don't know why you're quitting. This is nonsense.' So many times you've explained to Nanny. It was easier to go along at first, but now you realize the problem with that.

You tell her it's the end of the school year and you might go back in the fall but you're not sure yet. You say there's been some conflict among the faculty members over trash in the classrooms. 'I don't know what to do,' you say. You ask for money to buy a plane ticket. You tell her she can send it to the same address she sends the letters. She says she has to get the dog off of her lap. 'I have an ink pen right here,' she says. You've given her the address four other times, but you tell her again. She says, 'Why on earth would I mail a cheque to someplace in Texas, Ricky? That doesn't make any sense to me.' You get the dreadful feeling that maybe she chooses her moments of sanity. Nanny says that Ashley is going crazy over something in the kitchen, probably a mouse behind the refrigerator. She has to get off the phone to see what the ruckus is about. 'I can't have her hurting herself. They're all I've got, Ricky. These sweet little dogs.' She hangs up and for a while you keep the receiver to your ear, listening to the droning static of the open line until the guard taps on the door to say your time is up.

After dinner you and Donald play cards and drink milk, sharing the same styrofoam cup, taking little sips so that there is always another drink left. You always do it this way when you have milk before bed, and there is always one last sip. Even before the lights are turned off you put your hands down the front of Donald's underwear. You hold his penis. Donald punches you in the arm and then puts his hand in your underwear too. He tries jacking you off. You each hold the other's penis. Donald doesn't know what he's doing. He gets too rough. You think he's trying to make it hurt. You don't say it hurts though and, eventually, it starts to feel good.

The lights go out before you're done.

'Stay here,' he says.

'Where?'

'Here, idiot. With me.'

'I don't think I can.'

'Then do something,' he says, smiling.

'What do you mean?'

'I already said.'

You get in Donald's bed. He puts his head under the cover. Puts you in his mouth. He bites you. You're wishing you knew how to help him. You're wishing he knew what he was doing, that he meant it. His teeth get in the way. He's going too fast. 'Are you close?' he says.

'I think so,' you say.

He moves around for a few minutes. He presses his thumbs into your thighs. Eventually he gives up, slides back on to the pillow and props his head on an arm. He uses his other hand on you. He stares at you while he does it. He's never let you be this close to his face but after a minute he is finally putting his lips close to yours, easing his tongue in your mouth. He opens too wide and breathes across your teeth until you are running out over his knuckles and down on to your stomach. He's right there in front of you and you can feel his mouth widening into a smile. Something shifts, spreads through your body like a vivid fluid crowding out your limbs.

'You don't want to leave,' he says. 'I've got fifteen more years of this fucking place. Think about that.'

'Eleven,' you say. 'You've got eleven more years.'

'Yeah,' he says. 'Eleven. That's what I meant.'

'Why?'

'I ran over a dog.'

'Did the dog belong to someone famous?'

'No. Moron.' He's quiet. He sits up, then lies down again. 'Do you have kids?' he says.

'You know I don't.' It's like he's forgotten who he's even talking to.

'That's right, you don't. They're not what you expect. It's not like how you imagine. You think you can look at someone else's kids and know what it's like.' Donald lets down his ponytail. The hair falls forward, hiding his face. 'When they're yours it's like they're wild animals or something and you have to clean up their shit and keep them from burning the house down or running into the street during traffic.'

You want to get up. 'I should sleep,' you say.

Donald grabs you. 'You're a fucking moron, Ricky.'

'No, I'm not.'

'You're like every other motherfucker in here.'

You're thinking he's going to hit you. You get up but he just sits there with his hair in his eyes. 'Why are you like the way you are?' you ask, but he doesn't talk now. You reach out to touch him, but you smack him instead, without even thinking, across the face. You hit him in the head, and arms, then on the chest. You're right up on him and both of your arms and hands are throbbing with the way it feels to touch him like this. You're on top and he's on the bed and you're trying to give him what he wants. He's yelling. He wants it to hurt. He wants it to bad. He's covering his face and moving towards the wall and pretending. He's doing you a favour. He's saying you're crazy, someone help, you're fucking nuts. The door opens and the guard is saying, 'Ricky, get off. Back up!' The guard is in the room and he's bending your arms behind you. He is pushing you out and holding your wrists against the middle of your back as he leads you into the long, loud hallway of men who are watching and whistling as you go by.

He takes you out of the cell block and into a room with pictures on the walls. There are chairs all around, like in a waiting area. Another guard drags one of the chairs towards the middle and handcuffs you to it. You're in there alone for a long time, sitting in the chair, with a fiery and disordered ache still in your arms and face. Every so often you can hear the sound of something mechanical, an engine of some kind on the other side of the wall. There are shelves filled with magazines and thick paperbacks, and a small window, high up, with a white curtain. It is different in here, not like the rest of the prison. It is for employees, you think. That you're handcuffed to the meagre chair seems like a joke.

Eventually you hear the door, and the guard comes, with two little cups. 'Here,' he says. One of the cups is full of water, and the other has a pill in the bottom, something small and yellow, and unfamiliar. 'I can't,' you say. 'I can't take it.'

'Yeah, you can. It's fine.' He sounds bored, like he's said this before. 'I promise. Just swallow it. It's so you can sleep.'

Stare at the pill, and then the guard. Recall the distant rapture of pharmaceuticals. 'People get nervous, Ricky. You're a kid. Shit is scary. Take the pill.'

Dump the pill out of the cup into your hand and put it in your mouth. Drink the water and swallow. The guard says to stand up and come with him. He walks you out of the room, down another hall into a different cell where there's just a cot and a toilet. This is the hole. You know it once you're inside. The door is closed and then it's too dark to see. You feel your way around. The guard says he'll see you later. You find the cot and lie down and think about Nanny for a long time until, finally, you're seized by the miraculous buoyancy of the little pill. After that, there's not much.

There is a long corridor of solid metal doors that eventually open to the prison yard, and then to an enormous parking lot, and beyond that the grass and the interstate where the cars pass all day long like birds migrating in both directions. In the morning no one talks about what happened. They give you a bus ticket and eighty-six dollars. 'For food,' the man says, after he explains how long the trip will take, and the various stops, on the way back to Indiana. They give you the same clothes you were wearing when you came in. You don't know how to feel about this. It's like you're supposed to walk out and pick up where you left off. You sit down on the floor and tie your shoes. You have forgotten about them. You see them on your feet and you're shocked by the way they look. A stocky lady wearing red lipstick and big sunglasses comes out from behind the desk she's sitting at and says, 'Come on, Ricky. I guess I'm taking you.' She talks into her radio. She says some numbers. You don't know what they mean. You follow her out of the door and to a car. You're not sure if you should open the car door yourself or wait for her to do it. She comes up behind you and puts her hand on your back and says, 'You can sit up front – if you want.'

You get in the front seat of the car. The interior is hot. It feels good against the backs of your legs. Go with her, down the service road, on to the interstate. It's a few miles to the bus stop where there's a sign in the window that reads, 'Give Us Your Hungry', which seems very silly to you. This is not prison. This is a bus stop. Here the shoe meets the grass. After she drives off, you stand there for a long time. If you wanted you could stare down at the gravel parking lot all day. This is where people get up from their seats any time they want and maybe even walk to the North Pole if they think there's something there worth walking to. It smells like dirt, and the bitter exhaust of so many buses. You're like John Smith, you think, or William Clark, or Amerigo Vespucci, an eager frontiersman plodding off towards the darkest places. ∎

GRANTA

'A terrific collection of stories - mostly true ones, about families,
mostly dysfunctional ones... All beautifully written'
William Leith, *Evening Standard*

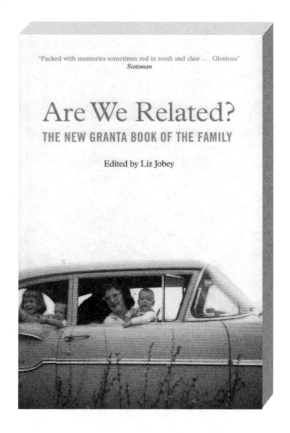

A wonderful montage of family relationships from the
past fifteen years of *Granta* magazine

Now in paperback

About the Cover

On the border between Nigeria and Libya. Illegal immigrants from Nigeria and South Niger flee their hunger-stricken homelands and cross into Libya on trucks, in the hope of finding work. The truck drivers often abandon them in the desert, several hundred kilometres from the nearest city, if they see any sign of border controls. The migrants are used to living in forests and are completely unprepared for the desert. 2001. RAYMOND ĐEPARDON/MAGNUM PHOTOS.

CONTRIBUTORS

Aravind Adiga was born in Madras in 1974. He was educated in New York and at Oxford. His new novel, *Last Man in Tower* (Atlantic/Knopf), will be published later this year. He lives in India.

Roberto Bolaño (1953–2003) won the National Book Critics Circle Award for his novel *2666* (Picador/FSG). 'Beach' is an extract from the upcoming collection, *Between Parentheses* (Picador/New Directions).

Adam Broomberg and **Oliver Chanarin** have been collaborating for over a decade. The recipients of numerous awards, including the Vic Odden Award from the Royal Photographic Society, they have produced six books and held exhibitions internationally. Their new book, *People in Trouble Laughing Pushed to the Ground*, will be published by Mack in February.

Afshin Dehkordi was born in Iran in 1975 and is a graduate of University College London and Harvard University. His critically acclaimed work has been exhibited across the UK and abroad. He lives in London and works for the BBC Persian Service.

Chris Dennis grew up in southern Illinois. He holds an MFA in Fiction from Washington University in St Louis, where he also received a postgraduate fellowship. 'Here Is What You Do' is his first published story.

Mark Gevisser is the author of *A Legacy of Liberation: Thabo Mbeki and the Future of the South African Dream* (Palgrave Macmillan). He is the Writing Fellow at the University of Pretoria in South Africa.

Juan Felipe Herrera recently received a National Book Critics Circle Award in Poetry and a 2010 Guggenheim fellowship. His next book is a young-adult novel, *SkateFate* (Rayo).

Robert Macfarlane's books include *Mountains of the Mind* (Granta Books/Vintage) and *The Wild Places* (Granta Books/Penguin). He is currently completing a book on paths, walking and the imagination.

Dinaw Mengestu is the author of the novels *The Beautiful Things that Heaven Bears* (Riverhead, published in England as *Children of the Revolution*, Jonathan Cape) and *How to Read the Air* (Jonathan Cape/Riverhead). He is the recipient of the Guardian First Book Award, and one of the *New Yorker*'s '20 under 40' writers to watch.

Nami Mun currently lives and teaches in Chicago. Her debut novel, *Miles from Nowhere* (Virago/Riverhead), was shortlisted for the Orange Prize for New Writers.

Philip Oltermann grew up in Schleswig-Holstein, and is now an editor at the *Guardian*. He is currently writing a book about Anglo-German encounters for Faber.

Julie Otsuka is the author of the novel *When the Emperor Was Divine* (Penguin/Knopf). 'Come, Japanese!' is an excerpt from her forthcoming novel, *The Buddha in the Attic* (Knopf).

Ann Patchett is the author of six novels and two works of non-fiction, including *Bel Canto* (Fourth Estate/Harper), which won the PEN/Faulkner Award and the Orange Prize, and *Run* (Bloomsbury/Harper). Her new novel, *State of Wonder* (Bloomsbury/Harper) will be published in June.

Paul Theroux is the author of the highly acclaimed *The Elephanta Suite* (Penguin/Houghton Mifflin Harcourt), *Dark Star Safari* (Penguin/Houghton Mifflin Harcourt), *Riding the Iron Rooster* (Penguin/Mariner), *The Great Railway Bazaar* (Penguin/Mariner), *The Old Patagonian Express* (Houghton Mifflin Harcourt), *Ghost Train to the Eastern Star* (Penguin/Mariner) and, most recently, *A Dead Hand* (Hamish Hamilton/Mariner).

Madeleine Thien is the author of *Simple Recipes* and *Certainty* (Faber/Little, Brown & Co.). McClelland & Stewart in Canada will publish her new novel, *Dogs at the Perimeter*, from which 'James' has been excerpted, in May.

Binyavanga Wainaina is a Bard Fellow and the Director of the Chinua Achebe Center for African Literature and Languages at Bard College. His forthcoming book, *One Day I Will Write About This Place: A Memoir*, will be published by Graywolf Press and Granta Books this year.

Natasha Wimmer has translated Roberto Bolaño's *2666* (Picador/FSG) and *Antwerp* (Picador/New Directions). Her translation of Bolaño's essay collection *Between Parentheses* will be published this year (Picador/New Directions).

Adam Zagajewski's new collection, *Unseen Hand*, will be published in June by FSG. Born in Lvov, Poland, he now lives in Chicago and Krakow.

Contributing Editors
Daniel Alarcón, Diana Athill, Peter Carey, Sophie Harrison, Isabel Hilton, Blake Morrison, John Ryle, Lucretia Stewart, Edmund White.

GRANTA 114: WINTER 2011 | EVENTS

Aliens on Paradise Row
14 February, 6.30 p.m.
Paradise Row Gallery, 74 Newman St.,
London W1T 3EL
A discussion with photographers Adam
Broomberg and Oliver Chanarin, with
a reading of Nami Mun's story 'The
Anniversary'.

The Participant and the Observer
15 February, 6.30 p.m.
Brunei Suite, SOAS, London WC1H 0XG
Deputy Editor Ellah Allfrey in conversation
with Mark Gevisser and Dinaw Mengestu.
In association with the Royal African Society.

London, That Strange Place*
16 February, 6.30 p.m.
19 Princelet St., London E1 6QH
Join Philip Oltermann and others to discuss
immigrants' experiences of London. In
support of the Museum of Immigration and
Diversity.

Aliens Launch Party in London
17 February, 6.30 p.m.
Daunt Books, 83 Marylebone High St.,
London W1U 4QW
Readings and discussion with *Granta* 114
contributors.

Aliens at Polari
18 February, 7.45 p.m.
Southbank, London SE1 8XX
Join Mark Gevisser for Paul Burston's
literary salon. With Christopher Fowler,
Rebecca Chance, Oliver Fritz, Paul Harding
and Lois Walden.
http://www.southbankcentre.co.uk.

Aliens Launch Party in Chicago
24 February, 7 p.m.
Barbara's Bookstore at UIC, 1218 South
Halsted St., Chicago, IL 60607
With Chris Dennis and Nami Mun. Hosted
by *Granta* writer Stuart Dybek.

Aliens Launch Party in Brooklyn*
24 February, 7 p.m.
The Brooklyn Art Library
103A N. 3rd St., Brooklyn, NY 11211
Julie Otsuka and Binyavanga Wainaina
discuss their work at this launch event for
our digital art project, 'I Am an Alien'.

Aliens Launch Party in Paris*
24 February, 7 p.m.
Village Voice Bookstore, 6 Rue Princesse,
75006 Paris
Mark Gevisser and Dinaw Mengestu discuss
their work.

Aliens Launch Party in Toronto*
24 February, 7 p.m.
Type Books, 883 Queen St. West, Toronto,
M6J 1E9
With Madeleine Thien.

Alien Voices: Identity and Writing
25 February, time TBC
The New School, 66 West 12th St., New
York, NY 10011
With Julie Otsuka and Binyavanga Wainaina.

Aliens in Salinas*
27 February, all-day event
National Steinbeck Center, One Main St.,
Salinas, CA 93901
During John Steinbeck's birthday
celebrations, the NSC hosts an Aliens
photobooth. Visitors are welcome to submit
their response to the statement, 'I Am an
Alien'.

Aliens Launch Party in New York City
28 February, 7 p.m.
McNally Jackson Books, 52 Prince St., New
York City, NY 10012
With Julie Otsuka and Binyavanga Wainaina.

*These events are part of our viral project,
'I Am an Alien'.